The Loin King

The Loin King

366 Sexy and Uplifting Aphrodisiacs to Answer the Call of the Wild

Ryan O'Horn

adams
media

AVON, MASSACHUSETTS

Published by Adams Media
an F + W Publications Company
57 Littlefield Street
Avon, MA 02322

ISBN 10: 1-59869-437-5
ISBN 13: 978-1-59869-437-6

Printed and bound in China

This book is available at quantity discounts
for bulk purchases. For information, please
call 1-800-289-0963.

Visit our home page at www.adamsmedia.com

This book was conceived,
designed, and produced by
iBall, an imprint of Ivy Press
The Old Candlemakers
West Street, Lewes
East Sussex, BN7 2NZ, England
www.ivy-group.co.uk

CREATIVE DIRECTOR Peter Bridgewater
PUBLISHER Jason Hook
EDITORIAL DIRECTOR Caroline Earle
ART DIRECTOR Sarah Howerd
SENIOR PROJECT EDITOR Hazel Songhurst
DESIGNER Simon Goggin
ILLUSTRATOR Emma Brownjohn
PICTURE RESEARCHER Katie Greenwood

Contents

Introduction

The history of aphrodisiacs goes back to when Eve offered Adam a nibble of her fruit in an attempt to arouse his interest. Since then, we've tried all sorts of recipes for overcoming the problems of flagging libidos and drooping desire.

The word "aphrodisiac" is derived from Aphrodite, the Greek goddess of love, who is often depicted rising naked from the waves on an oyster shell—so it's no surprise that seafood is high on the list of erotic foods. To the ancients, it was associations like this which gave many ingredients their libidinous reputation. Some animals were notorious for their sexual stamina and prowess, so eating their meat was also thought to endow the consumer with similar attributes. It was all part of the "Doctrine of Similars"—a system of treating

> While Venus fills the heart (without heart really
> Love, though good always, is not quite so good),
> Ceres presents a plate of vermicelli—
> For love must be sustain'd like flesh and blood—
> While Bacchus pours out wine, or hands a jelly:
> Eggs, oysters, too, are amatory food.
>
> "DON JUAN," BY LORD BYRON, 1819

like with like—which included the idea that if something looked like male or female genitals, it would boost the sex drive.

Medieval herbalists and alchemists modified the theory to include substances that brought on orgasmic symptoms—sweating, racing pulse, breathlessness—and current medical science has jumped on the aphrodisiac bandwagon, too.

So make your choice from this exotic and erotic banquet. Each ingredient has a "call of the wild" rating so that you can adjust your input according to the desired output. And there are enough to keep you going every night of the year—plus one in reserve for a repeat performance.

Foods To Raise
The Dead

In the search for foods that can rekindle passions and sustain the necessary vigor, you'll come across a huge variety of choices. Some are delicious, some lubricious, most nutritious, and a few downright disgusting. Just about every category of foodstuff gets a mention, and the list of ingredients throws up some strange bedfellows—where else would you find bananas and goat's testicles lumped together?

1 Feeling Fruity

From the exotic durian to the humble potato, nearly every fruit and vegetable has, at one time or another, been considered an aphrodisiac. Mostly they've gained the reputation on account of their suggestive shapes or the luscious juiciness of their ripe flesh—I defy anybody to eat a banana or peel a peach without thinking even momentarily about sex. But there's a good scientific basis for choosing them to improve your love life: they're packed with the vitamins and trace elements that are essential to good sexual health.

Being the most obviously phallic of all fruits, bananas figure highly on everyone's list of aphrodisiac fruits. Just peeling back the skin and biting into the firm flesh is an almost indecent act—and slicing them into a bowl is verging on the sadistic. Not only that, they're chock-full of potassium and B vitamins, which are essential for producing sex hormones, and some think that the bromelain enzyme in them improves male libido.

Under the Covers

Islamic mythology tells us that Adam and Eve, after their fruity feast with the serpent, covered their nakedness with banana leaves rather than fig leaves. Perhaps they had more to hide than we thought ...

3 Life's A Peach

In distinct contrast to the banana, peaches and their near-relatives, nectarines, are distinctly feminine. The curvaceous cleft fruit has reminded more than one poet of quite another kind of cleavage, and the soft, fuzzy skin—which even appears to blush—and juicy insides have done much to enhance its erotic connotations.

Nectar Of The Gods
"A nectarine—Good God, how fine. It went down all pulpy, slushy, oozy—all its delicious embonpoint melted down my throat like a large, beatified strawberry." *John Keats*

The apricot was originally known in English as "apricock," a misnomer if ever there was one. Like the peach, it has long symbolized femininity because of its supposed resemblance to a woman's genitalia. Both the fruit and essential oils extracted from the tree are said to have a calming and relaxing effect, which can put the user in a languid loving mood.

Fit For A King

Packed with vitamins, oranges have been renowned for their stimulating qualities since antiquity, especially the carnal-looking blood oranges and suggestive navel variety. However, their popularity as an aphrodisiac soared in seventeenth-century England when King Charles II took as his mistress an orange-seller called Nell Gwyn. The clincher was that the fruits she sold were reputed to be reminiscent of her other charms.

The ancient Greeks and Romans revered the grape as a symbol of all things sensual—and not just because it was the source of their favorite tipple, wine. The Greek god of wine, Dionysus—called Bacchus by the Romans—was often portrayed eating grapes, and he was also the god of procreation and fertility, so it's not surprising that grapes were thought to be sexy. They're perfect for couples to feed to one another, too, either as finger food or nibbled from the vine.

"Come Up And See Me Some Time …"

Mae West is famous for some of the most erotic lines in cinema history. Perhaps the most decadently suggestive is in the 1933 movie *I'm No Angel*, when she says to her maid, "Beulah, peel me a grape."

A Buxom Pear

The adjective "callipygian," meaning having beautiful buttocks, doesn't often spring to mind, but it could have been coined specially to describe the voluptuous pear. But there's only a short time to enjoy the succulent fruit and its sweet aroma at its passion-inflaming best: bite in too early and you'll meet gritty resistance; too late and the heart's turned to mush. Sound familiar?

Most of us associate the apple with the temptation of Eve in the Garden of Eden, and think of it as the ultimate forbidden fruit. Perhaps that's why, in medieval Europe, it was the focus for the amorous antics that took place every fall to celebrate the harvest and ensure a good crop the following year. Even in ancient Greece apples were linked to loving—tossing an apple to someone was considered to be an invitation to more intimate nibbles.

The Apple Of Your Eye

There's a belief in certain parts of Germany that the surest means of seduction is to eat an apple soaked in perspiration from the armpit of the object of your desires. Just how you're supposed to do that if you haven't managed to get that close before is not made clear.

9   Ma Cherie

The English language is littered with cheeky references to cherries, from women with lips like cherries to girls losing theirs. And, of course, the fruit's similarity to a nipple cannot be overlooked—particularly when on top of a cake or ice-cream sundae. More than that, they contain substances such as potassium and antioxidants that may help ensure a healthy sex life, and their musky scent is believed to stimulate the production of pheromones (see page 330).

In all its many varieties—cantaloupe, galia, charentais, and especially muskmelon and the horned type—the melon positively oozes fragrant sexuality. The word is practically a synonym for breast in many countries, and melons have been prized as potent aphrodisiacs since classical times. Watermelons, although they are, in fact, more closely related to cucumbers than to true melons, are even more juicily sensuous.

Choosy Fruit

An apocryphal proverb from South America puts the melon's erotic charms in startling perspective: "A woman for duty, a boy for pleasure, but a melon for ecstasy."

11 Go, Man, Go!

In India, the world's largest mango-producing country, the mango is both a symbol of love and something of a panacea. It is reputed to be a good antiseptic, expectorant, laxative, digestive aid, and much more besides, but is most often prescribed to women as a contraceptive and to men to improve flagging virility.

Man-go Or Woman-go

Strangely, while the Indians think of the mango as resembling a woman's breast, in Southeast Asia it is considered to be symbolic of manhood. Probably, given the shape and size of most fruits, that's just wishful thinking.

Cut a ripe papaya—aka pawpaw—lengthwise in two, and the soft pink flesh forms two lip-like curves around the seed cavity in the middle. It also has a rich, sweet, musky smell with erotic overtones—hardly surprising, as the fruit contains estrogenic compounds that are similar to female hormones. In the tropics, where it is native, it has been used to cure many feminine complaints, including lack of libido. An added bonus is it tastes great, too!

13 Hunky Chunks

Like most fruits, pineapples are full of vitamins—especially vitamin C—but in addition, they contain the enzyme bromelain, which is thought to increase male libido. Some homeopathic cures for impotence have a pineapple base, so there could be some foundation for this belief. So, for a delicious aphrodisiac treat that really stiffens your resolve, try sprinkling a spear of pineapple with chili powder.

Eating a passion fruit—or to give it its more mundane name, grenadilla—is a truly sensuous experience: cut a small hole at one end of a ripe, wrinkled fruit, squeeze gently, and slowly suck out the fragrant seeds and juices, then tear open the skin to lick out any remaining goodies. If that doesn't get the juices flowing, nothing will.

Praise The Lord!

Actually, grenadillas got their nickname from quite another kind of passion. The plant was named for the Passion of Christ, mainly because the flower is said to have connections with Christianity: the number of petals, stamens, and sepals corresponding to the apostles, gospels, and the Holy Trinity.

15 *Seedy Sex*

With its profusion of seeds and its deep pink color, the pomegranate has been linked to fertility, love, and sex since ancient Egyptian times. They associated the fruit with Hathor, the goddess of love and dance—and beer!—and made potent wines and liqueurs from the juice. It's a deliciously sticky and messy fruit that can only be eaten with the fingers, which is possibly why it's recommended as an aid to lovemaking in the *Kama Sutra*.

An open fig is unmistakably reminiscent of intimate female organs, and has long been prized as an aphrodisiac—in Mediterranean countries eating a fresh fig while standing naked in front of a woman is considered the most erotic act imaginable. It could be that the forbidden fruit of the Garden of Eden was originally a fig, and that's why fig leaves are traditionally used to cover nakedness in paintings and statues.

I Don't Give A Fig

In many languages, the word for fig is also a slang term for the vagina, and the offensively obscene gesture made by pushing the thumb between the fingers of a fist is also known as a fig in many Mediterranean countries. More evidence of the fruit's potency!

17 Figging The Ham

Fresh figs are great on their own or with a little cream but can also be used in combination with other dishes to add sweetness. You can make a luscious starter by decorating prosciutto with alternating slices of fig and melon or pear.

Poach two whole pears in sweet white wine flavored with a good dash of lime juice and a couple of split vanilla pods. When they're just soft, remove them from the liquid, peel and halve them. Add some sugar or fruit syrup—agave syrup would be ideal—to the remaining liquid and bring to the boil until it reduces and caramelizes. Pour over the pears and decorate with vanilla pods.

Creamy Dip

Strawberries could owe their
reputation as amatory aids to
their heart shape, especially
when halved, and the inevitable
suggestion of Valentine and Venus.
A less innocent explanation is that
they're also bulbously phallic, and
the effect is enhanced when they're
dipped in cream. Either way, the French
especially consider them the food of
love, and have a tradition of serving cold
strawberry soup to newlyweds to make
their wedding night one to remember.

Given its shape and dusky pink coloring, "fruit nipple" is a pretty good description of a raspberry. But beware! Appearances may be deceptive—despite their luscious appearance, raspberries are considered by some to actually cool your ardor.

... And Two For Tease

Raspberries are the perfect finger food for lovers—sweet, succulent, and bite sized. To give added frisson to placing them between your lover's lips, push your fingertip into the cavity inside the berry, dip in sugar or cream, and offer them one at a time.

Firm And Fruity

Because it is rich in pectin, quince made into a conserve sets to a firm consistency when other fruits would simply reduce to a quivering jelly. The resulting confection, known in Tudor times in England as quince marmalade, was touted as a surefire remedy for other things that needed firming up, and gave rise to the term "marmalade madams" for the prostitutes of the period.

What A Beauty!
In ancient Greece and Rome, the quince was dedicated to Aphrodite and Venus, the goddesses of love. Legend has it that the Trojan War was started when Paris was bribed by Helen of Troy to name Aphrodite the winner of a beauty contest, and award her the prize of a quince.

On the face of it, there's not much to suggest the medlar has any aphrodisiac properties: it's an unattractive cousin of the pear, which has been compared to a dog's butt, and it's not considered ripe enough to eat until it has begun to rot. Still, one man's poison is another's meat, and it appears to inflame some people's appetites. In medieval English literature the medlar was used as a symbol of prostitution.

Here We Go...

... around the mulberry bush. In English-speaking countries, mulberries are more often associated with the children's nursery rhyme than nights of steamy lovemaking, but the Chinese have used this dark and moody fruit in their aphrodisiac concoctions for centuries. The rich mix of vitamins and antioxidants found in them may have something to do with their standing as a stimulant—or perhaps it's because the leaves are the staple diet of the sexy silkworm.

Against all the odds, the durian has built quite a reputation for inducing lust. The creamy flesh is irresistibly delicious, but unfortunately far from fragrant—unless you've actually smelled a ripe durian, you can't begin to appreciate how unbelievably disgusting the odor is, somewhere between rotting corpses and pig manure. Anybody who can get it past their nose without gagging deserves more than just a tasty treat.

Room Service
Durian is so much sought after, both for its taste and its lubricious powers, that in Malaysia some hotel guests smuggle it into their rooms despite the ban imposed, understandably, by hoteliers who wish to keep the place smelling sweet.

Hot Date

A staple in the Middle East, dates are used by the Arabs as the basis of all kinds of medicinal treatments, not least to improve performance in the bedroom and increase fertility. The sweet and sticky fruits are high in calories and full of goodies such as potassium, calcium, and magnesium, so provide ample nutrition for even the most athletic lovers.

Love Food
It's not just the fruit of the date palm that gets the thumbs-up for boosting your sex life—the heart of the palm makes a libido-nourishing salad, the seeds give an oil believed to work as a contraceptive, and the pollen can be made into a brew that contains hormones similar to estrogen.

Whether you prefer them green or black, plain or stuffed, in oil or brine, olives make a sexily sophisticated starter to an erotic meal. In the Mediterranean, the health-giving fruit is revered as the way to achieve a long, happy, and fun-filled life—and who are we to argue with several million Latin lovers?

Not To Be Truffled With

Isabel Allende's book *Aphrodite* is a celebration of aphrodisiac foods. She tells one story of wanting to make a seductive truffle dish, but being unable to afford the expensive fungus. Chopped olives, marinated in truffle-scented oil were used as a substitute, and found to be "an infallible aphrodisiac."

Of course, any of the fruits we've looked at can be eaten on their own, but, just like people, they're often more exciting when they come together. A combination of mainly tropical fruits makes for a pretty potent fruit salad: try tossing together chunks of chilled fresh pineapple, slices of banana, halved strawberries, and whole raspberries, then squeeze the juice of a few passion fruit over it all. Serve immediately—you won't be able to hold back anyway.

Not a dish for the faint-hearted this one—but then faint heart never won fair lady, they say. Tomatoes are traditionally served as a vegetable, but they're far more exotically erotic if treated as the fruit they really are. Slice a couple of nicely ripe tomatoes into a bowl, then sprinkle with sugar and cover liberally with cream. Go on, take your lover by surprise!

Having A Ball

The Aztecs called the avocado *ahuacatl*, or "testicle tree," as the fruit hangs from the branches in provocative pairs, and because of this resemblance they thought it a powerful aphrodisiac. The Aztec sauce *ahuaca-mulli* was made by mashing the fruit, sometimes with onions, tomatoes, and cilantro, and is the origin of guacamole— sexier than filling it with prawn cocktail, unless you're planning a 1970s-style wife-swapping party.

Deny Everything

The avocado's reputation continues to the present, perhaps thanks to a clever advertising campaign in the USA in the 1920s, denying that there was any truth in the rumor that it could improve your love life. Needless to say, the campaign was successful—sales immediately rocketed.

The tomato's standing in the ranks of aphrodisiacs is a distinctly shaky one. Although it has often been called "love apple," this is probably a sixteenth-century misunderstanding. The Conquistadors first brought the fruit to Europe, assuming it to be a variety of apple. In Italy it was called *pomo d'oro*—"apple of gold"—because of its then-yellow coloring, and also *pomo di Moro* for its Spanish origins, but this was misheard by the French as *pomme d'amour*, or "love apple."

The Fun Starts Here

Asparagus just has to be one of the sexiest vegetables around, and the phallic shape alone "stirs up lust in man and woman," as the herbalist Nicholas Culpeper once said. It is a must for any erotic dinner party, ideally served on its own as an hors d'oeuvre, liberally coated in butter. You'll find that eating them with your lover is a none too subtle indication of what way the evening is headed.

Just Coming

As well as high levels of vitamin E, asparagus contains more folic acid than most vegetables. Folic acid is thought to promote production of histamines, which have a beneficial effect on our ability to achieve orgasm. So come and try—or vice versa.

Cool As A Cu-cum-ber 32

Despite the obviously suggestive shape, you might
have thought that cucumber would do more to cool
a woman's ardor than inflame it, but you'd be wrong.
Recent research shows that the subtle cucumber scent
is a real turn-on for the ladies, stimulating increased
blood flow to the vagina. However, pickled cucumbers
and gherkins lose that sexy aroma, and as an erotic
food they really don't cut the mustard.

What's Up, Doc?

Carrots: rabbits eat them, for goodness sake—and we know what they get up to, and how much—so they must be good for getting things going, right? Well, you wouldn't be the first to think so. The firm, distinctly virile-looking carrot has always been thought of as a remedy for a sagging masculinity, and was used by Middle Eastern royalty to give reluctant members some encouragement.

In A Rut

The Roman Emperor Caligula was notorious both for his sexual appetite and his lunatic behavior. Believing carrots to be the most potent aphrodisiac, he fed the Senate a banquet of nothing but carrot dishes in the hope that he could then watch them "rutting like wild beasts."

Like so many foods for the would-be fornicator, leeks have a long history of erotic usage. Ancient Greeks and Romans believed they had magical powers to invigorate virility, and the musically inclined Emperor Nero is said to have eaten a plate of leek soup every day—to improve the quality of his voice, he maintained, but his mind was probably on a completely different kind of performance.

35 _A Seminal Soup_

Not everyone loves leeks, but they can be made into one of the most voluptuous of all soups, vichyssoise. Using only the white part of the leeks, softened in butter, puréed with steamed potatoes, thickened with cream, and seasoned with salt and pepper, the soup should be chilled for an hour before serving.
The taste, texture, and color are bound to get the love juices flowing, especially if you believe in the Doctrine of Similars _(see Introduction)_.

Just as a fruit salad brings together a variety of stimulating ingredients, ratatouille is a mixture of the most invigorating vegetables in a sultry Mediterranean tomato sauce. Chunks of zucchini, eggplant, onions, and sweet peppers sautéed in olive oil are then simmered in chopped tomatoes and Provençal herbs to make the classic ratatouille—but try adding a few olives or mushrooms for a really powerful love potion.

Seed Or Stalk?

There's a real difference of opinion between East and West over the use of celery in the aphrodisiac recipe book. Europeans and Americans favor the stalk to fortify their manhood, while in Asia it is the celery seeds that are used to encourage a loving relationship between the sexes. The Asians may be right, as it's often said that eating a stick of celery uses more energy than it provides.

Sweat Success

Celery has recently been found to contain the male hormone androsterone, which may be released in the sweat after digestion. The virtually odorless hormone is subliminally detected by women who find it irresistibly attractive. Apparently.

Garrison Keillor, the chronicler of Lake Wobegon, describes rhubarb pie as the "secret aphrodisiac of the Midwest." It's a pretty well-kept secret, and probably with good reason. Although rhubarb contains oxalic acid, which is present in other love foods such as chocolate, the Romans treated its arousing power with caution, as it's also a strong laxative—so you may not know whether you're coming or going.

Eat Your Greens!

There's something inherently unsexy about green vegetables. But it wasn't always like that—Tiberius, the Roman Emperor, warned his son to lay off the broccoli after he heard he'd had his way with nearly all the slaves in the palace.

Sour Is Sweet
Only marginally racier than plain boiled greens, you might think, is sauerkraut. However, research in the USA indicates that eaten in quantity this cabbage-and-vinegar concoction actually does beef up the male libido.

If you subscribe to the Doctrine of Similars *(see Introduction)*, then cauliflower is more likely to be considered a food for the brain than the amatory organs— as Mark Twain once remarked, cauliflower is "just cabbage with a college education." But some might say the brain is the sexiest organ of all, and Rasputin downed vast quantities of pickled cauliflower to fuel his voracious sexual appetite.

Sweet Patooties

Sir Walter Raleigh first brought the potato to Elizabethan England, but some time before that sweet potatoes had been known as an aid to conjugal bliss. Bishop Andrewe Boorde, in his *A Compendyous Regyment on a Dietary of Helth*, wrote that "they both increase nature and doth provoke a man to veneryous actes." He should know: he was later unfrocked and jailed for keeping prostitutes in his rooms.

It has been said that you don't so much eat an artichoke as undress it, and there's definitely something risqué about stripping off the tough outer leaves and sucking the soft flesh from their stems. To be honest, though, apart from their hearts, there's not a lot of goodness to be had from them, and it is probably the process rather than the nutrition that lubricates the lust.

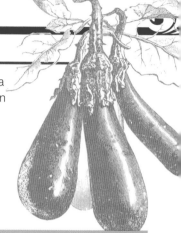

43 Egging You On

The eggplant was named after a white, egg-shaped variety grown in England—and that may be at the bottom of why so many people associate it with fertility and lustful urges, along with its rich, soft, and fleshy texture when cooked.

Rubbing It In

The Indian guide to lovemaking, the *Kama Sutra*, mentions the eggplant in glowing terms. As well as recommending it as an aphrodisiac food, it says that you can boost your lover's libido by rubbing the juice of the fruits into their skin.

No awards for guessing how the zucchini made it to this hit list—but why its big brother the marrow doesn't is a bit of a mystery. Also known as courgettes, zucchini are a versatile vegetable that pack a potent punch, sexually speaking. And zucchini flowers have the same effect, apparently, especially when deep fried with a spicy stuffing.

A Helping Hand

Whichever way you look at it, okra's a pretty provocative
vegetable. Depending on your preferences, it either
resembles the delicate digits that give it its other name—
lady's fingers—or the male member it's reputed to stimulate.
And with its asparagus-like flavor and slippery, oozy texture
when cooked, it makes a sensual side dish or essential
addition to that most luscious of dishes, gumbo.

Lift Off 46

It might look like a sophisticated lettuce, but the peppery arugula has quite the opposite effect. Where lettuce is reputed to dampen the sexual spirits and put you to sleep, arugula lives up to its other name: rocket. The leaves are used to put a kick into salads, and the seeds and their oil can be used as a garnish to launch you into a steamy feast.

Keep It Up

The ancient Greeks recognized the explosively lustful potency of arugula. To mark the erection of statues of Priapus, the son of Aphrodite and Dionysus, with a legendary propensity for sustained arousal, they planted arugula seeds at its base.

Foods To Raise The Dead

55 ♥

Hard To Beet

Beet may not be most people's first choice of erotic vegetables these days, but there's growing evidence that it could help to put some color into your love life—it's rich in boron, which has a role in the production of sex hormones.

Beet That

A beet farmer from north England is cashing in on renewed interest in his crop since he claimed to have found evidence that the Romans used it as an aphrodisiac. On holiday on Pompeii, he noticed a beet depicted in a mural on an ancient brothel wall that was clearly not there for culinary purposes.

Next time you have a summer salad, try adding a few hot and peppery radishes to spice things up a bit. The ancient Egyptian Pharaohs thought they were a gift from the gods that would get to the root of any sexual problems they might be having.

Rampant Rutabaga

Turnips come in all shapes and sizes, and have various names such as swede and rutabaga, none of them particularly appetizing. But their unappealing looks and bland flavor are deceptive—in the Middle East, they are considered to be a quick fix for a lackluster love life.

The Root To Pleasure

Recent scientific research has rediscovered the restorative power of the turnip, or at least one variety of it. Maca *(see page 267)* is derived from a member of the turnip family, and is being widely used to put life back into members of the human family.

Looking like a cross between a carrot and a turnip, the parsnip at least has a suggestively elongated shape, but it is not believed to have quite the same potency as either. It was, apparently, confused with the carrot in classical times, presumably by colorblind cooks with jaded palates. Diners expecting to rise from their meal to some postprandial pranks probably went home disappointed.

51   A Fun Guy

Just take a look at a young mushroom before the cap is fully formed, and you'll see how they got to be the aphrodisiac of choice all over the world. Some, like the delicious morel, retain their thrusting phallic shape into maturity. But they're not just good lookers, they contain all sorts of trace elements essential for maintaining a healthy sex life, and are rich in glutamic acid, which is especially helpful in boosting the male libido.

Fungi have been associated with mystical rites at least since the time of the Etruscans nearly 3,000 years ago, and their magical power is often linked to their potency as aphrodisiacs. The centaurs of classical mythology were thought to have achieved their prowess in rutting from grazing on mushrooms, and some scholars reckon that ambrosia, the food of the gods, was a mushroom concoction.

Hard To Imagine

Many varieties of mushroom that rouse the passions are also hallucinogenic, and some, such as the powerfully priapic fly agaric, *Amanita muscaria*, are deadly poisonous. Not that that has stopped people using them to enhance their lovemaking. One way or another, however, they end up stiff.

Truffling With Your Affections

Truffles—no, not those chocolate confections, but the rare underground fungus hunted for with pigs, who find the smell irresistible—are both a gourmet's treat and a lover's delight. The French gastronome Anthelme Brillat-Savarin described them as making "women more amiable and men more amorous," as the rich, mushroomy flavor and musky scent make human skin more sensitive and stimulate the amatory organs.

Better Than Sex?

The fourteenth-century Duke of Clarence, so the story goes, married a woman from Alba in Italy, an area renowned for its truffles. To prepare himself for his wedding night, he feasted on so many of them that he died in his sleep before he could put their reputation to the test.

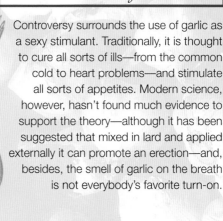

Controversy surrounds the use of garlic as a sexy stimulant. Traditionally, it is thought to cure all sorts of ills—from the common cold to heart problems—and stimulate all sorts of appetites. Modern science, however, hasn't found much evidence to support the theory—although it has been suggested that mixed in lard and applied externally it can promote an erection—and, besides, the smell of garlic on the breath is not everybody's favorite turn-on.

Know Your Onions

An essential ingredient in most entrées, onions are almost universally acclaimed as libido enhancers. In France, there was a tradition of serving onion soup to newlywed couples for the breakfast following their wedding night to replenish their depleted ardor.

Out Of Order

Many celibate religious orders—from the priests of ancient Egypt, through Tibetan Buddhist monks, the Jains and Brahmins of India, to medieval European friars—have forbidden their members onions, scallions, and garlic, all of which were thought to inflame the earthly passions.

The Roman epigrammatist Marcus Valerius Martialis—aka Martial—had plenty to say about both food and aphrodisiacs. He was a great fan of onions, especially the small variety known as shallots, and suggested that for "young men whose members are exhausted, and not-so-young women suffering from lack of desire" shallots would do the trick.

57 Scallywags

Commenting on the symbolism of foods depicted in sixteenth-century Italian still-life paintings, contemporary writer Bartolomeo Pisanelli is unambiguous about scallions: "The scallion serves no other purpose than to incite the libido ... It is similar in nature to the onion, aids coitus, and generates gross and viscous humors ... Those who use it continually have a notable increase in sperm, and great readiness for the act of coitus."

The gladiolus—sometimes called the sword lily—is named for its sword-shaped leaves, *gladius* being Latin for sword. Once you get to thinking about swords and sheaths, the metaphor is pretty transparent, and it's small wonder that eating the roots of the plant gained a reputation for sharpening up a man's sexual standing.

Cunning Linguists

The so-called "language of flowers" confirms the aphrodisiac qualities of gladioli, as according to this system their meaning is "love at first sight."

A Kick In The Nuts

It's not really surprising that nuts are considered a symbol of fertility in many cultures—partly because they grow in such profusion on the trees, but more obviously because of their similarity to that most tender part of the male anatomy. In fact, in many languages, the word for nuts is also a slang term for testicles. But they're also packed full of nutrients that are necessary for sustaining good sexual health.

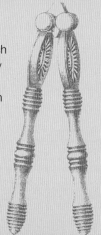

The sexiest-looking nut in the world—and, incidentally, the biggest seed pod, too—is the *coco de mer*. Shaped exactly like a curvaceous woman's pelvis and thighs, with even a shock of strategically-placed fuzzy hair, the fruit of the female plant—there are both male and female trees—can't help but be raunchy.

Love Islands

The *coco de mer* palm only grows on two of the 115 Seychelle islands in the Indian Ocean. Perhaps under the influence of the local nut, Seychelle islanders have a legendarily relaxed attitude to promiscuity.

When Samson was courting Delilah, he brought along branches of almond with fragrant blossoms, which were at that time considered a symbol of fertility and sexual power. And it's not just the flowers that he hoped would win her over—the smell of the nuts is supposed to provoke a woman to extreme passion, and eating them to drive her absolutely wild.

More than any other nut, the walnut—both its wrinkly shell, and the shriveled-looking nut within—resembles human "nuts," and as such has a reputation for increasing potency and desire. Ancient Romans threw them like confetti at newlywed couples as a symbol of fertility and sexual power.

By Jove!

Not everybody thinks of testicles when looking at a walnut. The Latin word for walnut is *juglans*, an abbreviation of *Jovis glans*, meaning the glans—head of the penis—of Jupiter, the chief among the Roman gods.

Monkey Business

Although not strictly a nut, the peanut—or ground nut, or monkey nut—is popularly said to have the same aphrodisiac efficacy as bonafide nuts, especially in South and Central America. In Brazil, for example, they make a tea from peanuts that calms and relaxes the drinker, putting him or her in the mood for love.

Buttering You Up

Peanut butter, about as American as apple pie, is practically a national institution. Maybe the stimulating power of the peanut explains the popularity of this innocent-looking spread with adults.

The Medicine Man's Man Medicine 64

Cola nuts, or kola nuts—however you spell it, these nuts have mystical properties. Throughout West and Central Africa, they are chewed or brewed into potent potions as magical medicine to pep up an ailing love life. However, there's a scientific basis for their reputation: they contain large quantities of stimulants such as caffeine, theobromine, and tannin.

65 Arabian Nuts

The Queen of Sheba knew a thing or two about the art
of love, and she rated pistachio nuts so highly for their
provocative potency that she reserved the crop of the best
Assyrian pistachios for herself and her royal guests.

Busting Out All Over

An Arabian folk story tells the tale of two lovers meeting one moonlit night
in a pistachio grove. The nuts were ripening, and as they sat they could hear
the sound of the shells bursting open. This was taken as an extremely good
omen, which led to good fortune and, presumably, a happy night of passion.

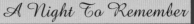

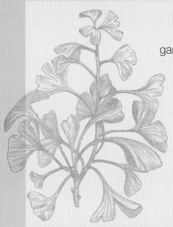

The ginkgo, or maidenhair tree, bears seeds containing nut-like gametophytes that are traditionally served at Chinese wedding feasts. Extracts from the ginkgo are believed to improve the circulation of the blood, especially boosting the flow to the genital organs. Increased blood flow also helps the memory, so the experience could be unforgettable.

Pining For Love

The Roman poet Ovid, the Greek medical scholar Galen, and the Arabian love manual *The Perfumed Garden* all recommend the use of pine nuts when a man's interest in love is beginning to droop. The high zinc content of the seeds found in pine cones is thought to help production of the necessary male hormones.

Despite their distinctly hirsute, macho appearance, coconuts are reputed to invigorate both men and women, providing energy and stimulating the hormones. Whether you prefer to sink your teeth into the firm white flesh, or suck out the milky juices, just remember to have some coconut first.

That's The Spirit

As well as their nuts and their milk, coconut palms yield another stimulating substance, the sap of the tree, which is known in some parts of the world as coconut wine. A spirit distilled from this juice, arak, is said to be potent in more ways than one.

Next time you're planning an evening of seduction, and pasta's on the menu, forget the meatballs and go for an erotic pesto. This classic Italian mix of sensual ingredients—basil, pine nuts, olive oil, garlic, and parmesan—is simple to prepare and never fails to please. Just toss the freshly cooked pasta in the sauce, ensuring it's evenly coated, and serve immediately.

Grinding It Together

The classic method of making pesto is, unsurprisingly, with a pestle and mortar. Grinding foods in this way has long been a metaphor for the desired outcome of a seductive meal, and should ideally be an activity undertaken with your partner.

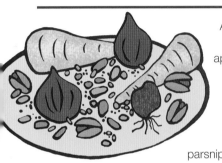

A side dish made from a combination of known aphrodisiacs was popular with the Romans from around the first century AD. It consisted mainly of grated gladiolus roots, orchid bulbs, and parsnips, to which were added crushed pine nuts and pistachios, and a sprinkling of arugula seeds. Given the reputation of every one of the ingredients, it must have been an explosive mixture.

A Racing Pulse

Pulses and grains are often thought to be the also-rans of the aphrodisiac larder, and they don't figure highly in many people's list of lusty ingredients. There are a few notable exceptions, however. In classical times Hippocrates and Aristotle both swore by lentils to maintain their manhood, and the poet Plutarch recommended bean soup.

Fassolatha, a sort of bean soup, is practically the national dish of Greece, where its inflammatory effect is legendary. Its ability to provoke the passions dates back to the classical period, when bean flowers were a symbol of sexual satisfaction.

It's A Gas

It may well be true that a hearty meal of beans can lead to a raunchy romp, but you could get more than you bargained for. Even if you take them in moderation, they also have an unfortunate side effect, possibly the ultimate passion-killer—flatulence.

Soy and its derivatives—including tofu, miso, and soy sauce—have recently gained a reputation for their aphrodisiac qualities, mainly by vegetarians trying to encourage the rest of us away from our carnivorous diet. They may well be right, but in Japan these foods are traditionally thought to cool overheated organs, and are used by monks to subdue their sexual urges.

Country lore has it that feeding oats to
their—male—stock will improve their animals'
fertility, and young men are said to "sow their
wild oats" when they go out "wenching."
There is a grain of truth in the rumor—*Avena
sativa*, to use the Latin name, is said to free up
testosterone and improve libido. All the same,
it's hard to make a bowl of oatmeal sexy.

Don't Worry, Be Happy
Another possible reason why eating oats helps you "get your oats"
is that they are thought to have a calming effect on the nervous
system and remove any anxiety about underperformance.
The less you worry, the harder it gets.

Unlike other grains, sweet corn really looks the part, and even though there is little evidence that it will do much physically for your love life, it can be a sexy dish. Served on the cob, dripping with butter, it makes for a really erotic eating experience.

The Hard Sell

Corn flakes didn't go down well when they were first launched in the USA—at least, not until the makers surreptitiously spread a rumor that they could improve your performance in the bedroom, after which they sold like hot cakes.

You won't be surprised to learn that in the Far East rice is regarded as helping you to rise to the occasion, often in the form of rice wines such as sake *(see pages 102 and 208)*, but the practice of throwing rice at weddings in the West may hark back to some ancient belief in its procreative powers. Some varieties are more highly prized than others as aphrodisiacs—black rice, for instance, was reserved for the Emperor's use in imperial China, and known as "forbidden rice."

77 Canoodling

The erotic effects of pasta are mainly psychological,
or because of the ingredients in the sauce
you have with it, but that doesn't stop
it making a seductively sensuous
meal. Coming in all shapes and
sizes, many of them erotically
suggestive, cooked *al dente*, and
served in an oily sauce, it has a
deliciously lubricious texture.

Doggy-style
If you need a demonstration of how flirtatious spaghetti can be, have
another look at the dinner scene in Disney's animation *Lady and the
Tramp*—an object lesson in how to share a bowl of pasta and meatballs.

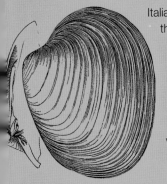

Italians have no doubts that pasta helps their legendary Latin love lives, and in coastal regions the sauce of choice is made with *vongole*, baby clams. Sauté onion and garlic in olive oil until tender, then add a good portion of clams and slowly stir in a little stock and a glass of white wine. Heat through and season with plenty of pepper—some like a bit of chili, too—then toss with whatever pasta you fancy—probably linguini, little tongues, being most appropriate.

Ever since Aphrodite rose from the waves on an oyster shell, seafood, especially shellfish, has been high up on the list of libidinous foods. Nearly all seafood is high in nutritious protein and trace elements that help with the hormones, and many have essential oils to keep you supple and lubricate the love machine.

Legend has it that Casanova ate fifty raw oysters every day to boost his libido. Occasionally, he chose to enjoy his *plat du jour* in a bathtub with his *femme du jour*. It's a wonder he was in the tub and not sitting on the toilet.

The Oyster Bed

The widely held belief in the aphrodisiac qualities of oysters may in part derive from their sexually suggestive texture and appearance—but they also contain high levels of zinc, which is needed for sperm production.

Mussel Man

If you can't afford oysters, or just can't get your hands on any—they're not available all year round—mussels make a pretty good substitute. Not only do they have just as many hormone-promoting goodies in them, when the shells part to reveal the fleshy lips inside they look even more foxily feminine than oysters.

Oysters and mussels aren't the only mollusks with a mighty reputation. There's a huge variety of shellfish, from cockles and clams to mussels and whelks, all of which excite the erogenous organs—which, come to think of it, most of them resemble in one way or another, too.

Alive, Alive—Oh!

In Dublin's fair city, so the song goes, the girls are so pretty, and a familiar sight was sweet Molly Malone, selling cockles and mussels from her barrow, most likely to the young bucks who need bracing up before trying to get in on the local action.

Getting Your Claws In

Ask any real gourmet which food satisfies the palate and stimulates the amorous appetites best, and the answer is invariably "lobster." Legendary lovers such as Casanova and Lothario would agree, and the priapic Gymnastes in Rabelais' *Gargantua* credits his prowess to ingesting large quantities of the bright-red beastie.

Never Miss A Trick
Lobsters also come with some professional endorsement. In the eighteenth century, the so-called "King of London's Streetwalkers," Mad William Windham, kept his girls doing brisk business by feeding them on lobsters and oysters.

Foods To Raise The Dead

Often thought of as poor-man's lobsters, crabs are just as naughtily nourishing. In fact, in countries bordering the Pacific Ocean, for stoking up the sexual fires crabmeat is preferred to that of lobsters. The famous Dungeness crab from the west coast of the USA is the main ingredient of the seductive Crab Louis—dressed crabmeat and hard-boiled egg, with a hot chili, cream, and mayonnaise sauce, laid on a bed of lettuce—and was a firm favorite with the singer and legendary ladies' man Enrico Caruso.

Size Isn't Everything

Except in Cantonese cookery, the aphrodisiac qualities of smaller crustaceans, such as shrimps and prawns, seem to get overlooked in favor of their bigger cousins, crabs and lobsters. Shame, because they're every bit as good for nourishing the libido—and peeling them with your fingers to get at the succulent tidbits is a suggestive and tactile delight.

Live And Let Live

Now, this isn't to be recommended—and its eroticism is dubious, to put it mildly—but apparently, in some parts of the Caribbean, islanders heighten their pleasure by eating live shrimps while making love. Whatever turns you on.

Anchovies are so strongly flavored, and perhaps so potently aphrodisiac, that they're seldom served on their own. Combined with other erotic ingredients in a puttanesca sauce for pasta, they're dynamite. The word *puttanesca* is Italian for in the manner of a whore, and the classic mix of anchovies, garlic, and chilies fried in oil and added to puréed tomato with chopped capers and olives is as wanton a sauce as you'll ever find.

Spanish Fry

Paella is a national dish in Spain, originating from the Valencia region. Traditionally cooked in a huge pan, the basic ingredients are rice, olive oil, and saffron, but it's the meaty garnish that gives it its aphrodisiac kick, including chorizo—a spicy sausage—chicken, and even snails, together with a potent mixture of seafood such as prawns, clams, crab, and especially lobster.

How Long Can You Keep It Up?
One famous version of paella was created by Casanova's companion, Angelo Torredana. As you would expect, lobster features in the recipe, and it must have worked for Torredana, as he is said to have died, aged ninety-two, while making love to his nineteen-year-old mistress.

Down in the south of France they reckon fish is the food to put you in the mood, and the soup known as bouillabaisse the best way to serve it. The active ingredient essential to an effectively libidinous bouillabaisse is the *racasse*—aka scorpion fish or rockfish—but it's traditionally made with whatever fish are on hand. These are boiled and reduced with onions, garlic, fennel, parsley, thyme, bay leaves, and orange rind, and then seasoned with pepper and saffron.

Although it wouldn't win any prizes in a beauty contest, the bug-eyed and land-loving mudskipper does have its attractions for some. Lovers in Kelantan, Malaysia, have discovered it really does pep up their sex lives. There's one small drawback: you have to eat the whole thing—live.

A lot of foods have earned their stimulating reputations simply because they're rare or expensive—if you can afford to offer them to your date you've immediately got the seductive edge. But luxurious caviar does more than just impress your potential partner, as it's rich in zinc and arginine, which help get the blood to the parts that matter.

Coming On Strong

Caviar is the roe, or eggs, of the sleek and powerful sturgeon. The fishy little black pearls are packed with protein, and the name caviar is from the Persian *khav-yar*, which means cake of strength.

A Flash In Japan

Japanese sushi is a comparative newcomer to Western tables, but it very soon established itself as a favorite, especially as an exotic prelude to an erotic performance. The dainty little nibbles are perfect for couples to share, the evocative colors and textures are provocative, too, but best of all its subtle combinations of energizing ingredients ensure men rise to the occasion admirably.

Fresh Fish

The stars of the sushi show are the variety of raw and lightly cooked seafood, renowned for working wonders with your love life—but don't forget the side dishes, including pickled ginger and the mind-blowingly hot wasabi *(see page 112)*, which spice up the evening no end.

One of the most popular fishes in Japan is the *unagi*, or eel, probably because of its celebrated libido-enhancing properties. There are even specialist *unagi* restaurants, signposted with the first letter of the word in Japanese hiragana script which represents the phallus-shaped fish.

Licensed To Kill

Before trying *fugu* at your local sushi bar, make sure the chef has a license to prepare it. Sushi chefs in Japan have to pass a rigorous exam, not just because this dish of Japanese puffer fish is reckoned to be one the great arousers of *amour* but more because it needs careful preparation to remove the poisons in some of its internal organs. It is literally a taste to die for, because a dose of bad fugu could get you stiffer than you'd bargained for.

Loving Spoonful

A particularly potent love potion, highly prized in Japan, is made by stirring a spoonful of fugu testes into a cup of hot sake. Have you got the balls to drink it, though?

There are hundreds of different varieties of sea cucumber found all over the world, and these elongated relatives of the sea urchin go by names ranging from bêche-de-mer to sea rat or even sea ginseng. What they all have in common, however, is their cucumber shape—or whatever your imagination wants to make of it!—and that they're eaten more for their passion-inducing qualities than their taste.

A Long Time Coming

Some love potions demand a bit of patience. Chinese recipes for shark's-fin soup typically involve several days of preparation, and the tough meat needs long, slow cooking. At the end of one recipe, which takes four days, the writer advises, "Eat, and await love's call." He doesn't say how long that might be, and we must assume that the results are worth the wait.

Fins Ain't What They Used To Be

If we are to believe an episode of *Xena: Warrior Princess*, Julius Caesar was a fan of shark's fin, too. When he was captured by Xena's pirates, he brewed up shark's-fin soup in an attempt to seduce her. Presumably he kept quiet about the supposed antidote, the liver of a torpedo ray.

Cephalopods—including the tasty squids, cuttlefish, and octopus—are recognized around the world as stimulants. The succulent flesh contains just as many aphrodisiac goodies as fish and shellfish, and, if cooked properly, needn't have the rubbery texture that you might expect. Several cultures also think that squid ink does the trick, too, and some recipes use it for rich, dark sauces.

Rooty-toot Sweet

The candied or pickled roots of the sea holly, *Eryngium maritimum*—known as eryngoes—were an aphrodisiac specialty of the east coast of England in Elizabethan times, supposed to be "good to be given to people that are consumed and withered with age," as the contemporary herbalist John Gerard coyly put it.

Sinning In The Rain

Shakespeare makes reference to eryngoes in *The Merry Wives of Windsor*, when Falstaff rails, "Let the sky rain potatoes ... hail kissing-comfits and snow eringoes, let there come a tempest of provocation," knowing his audience would catch the erotic implications of his choice of foods.

Glasswort—known in Britain as samphire—is regarded by herbalists as a cure for digestive problems, but for locals in the coastal regions of Europe and America where it grows in the salt marshes and mud flats, it is thought to get the sexual rather than the gastric juices flowing. Perhaps that's why it's known in some places as "sea asparagus."

Kelp In Times Of Trouble

The sea provides a rich crop of different plants, many of them highly nutritious. The brown seaweeds collectively known as kelp, for example, are chock-full of restorative vitamins and minerals, particularly iodine. This is essential to the proper working of the thyroid gland, which controls—among other things—our sex drive, so a side order of seaweed might reawaken your interest.

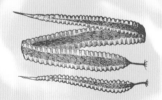

Seaweed can be found in many Asian dishes, from sushi to stir-fries, and is universally considered to kindle the passions. A favorite in Chinese restaurants is the crispy, deep-fried light-green seaweed served as a side dish—but beware, some unscrupulous cooks use cabbage or pak choi instead of the genuine article, and this will definitely not have the desired arousing effect.

When The Chips Are Down

Another crunchy seaweed nibble, a sexy alternative to potato chips, can be made by cutting brown oarweed into squares, drying them thoroughly and then deep-frying until they start to expand and go crisp. Guaranteed to stimulate the appetites.

101 The Spice Of Life

Often it's the little things in life that make it interesting, and that's just as true when it comes to food as it is in love. Herbs and spices are so potent in flavor and erotic effect that they aren't meant to be consumed in great quantities, but just added to dishes to give them zest. Good cooks know that you can transform a lackluster dish with a sprinkling of the right condiments, and many of them can spice up your love life, too.

Hot Stuff

Just as the Doctrine of Similars (*see Introduction*) suggests that a food that looks sexy must make you feel sexy, herbalists maintain that because any amorous activity increases the heart rate, raises the temperature, and causes sweating, herbs and spices that do the same must be aphrodisiac.

Cloves are used to flavor a variety of dishes, from apple pies to Indian curries, and their warming piquancy is believed to stir in particular the loins of the male of the species. Their name derives from the Latin *clavis*, meaning nail, which the clove bud resembles, and whose attributes of length, strength, and hardness are conferred on those who consume it.

103 *Good Clean Fun*

Herbalists recommend horseradish for invigorating and cleansing the system, clearing congestion, and improving the circulation—in particular to extremities that may be in need of beefing up. It's also pretty fiery, so probably helps to inflame the urges as well, but should only be taken in small doses.

Just Swell

Japanese horseradish, or wasabi, is even stronger stuff than the Western variety, but the real thing is difficult to come by, even in sushi restaurants. Women have been known to apply it externally to their mouths to achieve a full-lipped pout, and its power to induce swelling is not lost on the men.

Capsaicin is the active ingredient in chili peppers, and is responsible for the hotness of these potent little devils. It causes a burning sensation in the mouth, quickens the pulse, and provokes perspiration, but also acts as an irritant to the genitourinary system—which can stir up almost insatiable cravings.

If You Can't Stand The Heat

Cayenne pepper is a mixture of several different chili peppers, dried and ground to a powder. One of the hottest spices, it not only excites the senses but also, just like fresh chilies, causes the body to release endorphins that can bring about a state of blissful, relaxed well-being. No wonder it's highly prized as an adjunct to sex.

Currying Favor 106

India is, let's not forget, the land
that gave us the *Kama Sutra*, so
it's no surprise that Indian food
is almost without exception a
sensual treat. Recipes ranging
from the searingly hot vindaloo
to the mildest of kormas call for
spices that titillate the palate, and
at the same time awaken desires.

Lost In Translation

The subtle mix of spices in Indian foods must have seemed very exotic to
the soldiers of the British Raj, and they brought the erotic associations of
these back with them to the West. Strait-laced Victorians may have found
the spicy dishes too hot to handle so it took a while for curries to catch on.

Foods To Raise The Dead **115** ♥

After salt, pepper is probably the most widespread and commonly used seasoning, and it invigorates the body in much the same way as the other "hot" spices. In addition, it brings out the flavor of food to which it is added, and is thought to enhance the effects of any other aphrodisiac ingredients.

Mixing It

The Arab guide to lovemaking, *The Perfumed Garden*, contains references to the power of pepper; it recommends a mixture of pepper, cardamom, musk, galangal, honey, and ginger to drive a woman wild with lust. But don't try feeding this to your girlfriends, boys—it's for men to rub onto their skin.

Many of the pungent spices rely for their aphrodisiac effect on the blend of pain and pleasure they give, and with mustard there's a fine line between the two. You can opt for a mild American or French version, or the searingly hot English variety, according to taste—and how passionate you want to feel afterward.

Ginger was originally introduced into Europe as an aphrodisiac and not a culinary spice. Egyptian merchants made a killing selling it to the salacious Romans, with a sales pitch of how it cured impotence in the exotic East. To ginger things up, they used it externally as well as in their food.

Who Do Dolls?

Ever wondered why we eat gingerbread people? In medieval Europe, a maiden on the lookout for a lover would bake and then eat an effigy flavored with ginger of the man she was after.

All along the spice route from China to the West, nutmeg is prized for the warmth it imparts to lovemaking. It's not so much that it gets things going, but more because it is said to prolong the pleasure. But if you're looking for a night to remember, go easy on the nutmeg—eaten in large quantities it has a hallucinogenic effect.

111 Softly Seductive

The sweet aroma and soft flavor of vanilla give many sweet dishes a seductive charm, and are believed to be quite a turn-on, too. Adding a pod or two to your favorite dessert will give it a subtle sensuousness, and is bound to get a couple in the mood for love.

Simply Divine

A myth from Mexico tells of Xanat, daughter of the fertility goddess, and her love for a mortal man. Her divine status meant that their love could never be consummated, so she transformed herself into a vanilla plant that could give her lover the sensual happiness he had been denied.

Hand-picked stigmas of a species of crocus, three in each flower, are dried to make saffron, and it takes hundreds of thousands of them to produce just one pound of this subtly erotic flavoring and coloring, making it undoubtedly the most expensive spice. But it's worth the price, as it works by sensitizing the erogenous zones to intensify the ecstasy.

113 *King Solomon's Mine*

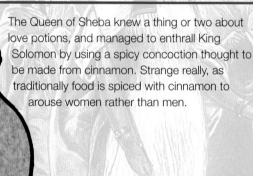

The Queen of Sheba knew a thing or two about love potions, and managed to enthrall King Solomon by using a spicy concoction thought to be made from cinnamon. Strange really, as traditionally food is spiced with cinnamon to arouse women rather than men.

♥122   Foods To Raise The Dead

The piquant leaves and pungent seeds of cilantro both work equally well in giving a kick in cooking and adding zest to a flagging love life. And there's no gender discrimination here either—apparently it has the same energizing effect on both sexes.

Inconceivable

Cilantro's provenance as an aid to male potency goes back a long way. There is a tale in the *Arabian Nights* of a couple who had been childless for forty years, but after taking a potion made from the plant the man succeeded in fathering a son.

115 | *Anise Candy*

The seeds of the anise plant have been hailed as lust inducers since classical times. Sucking on the tiny aniseeds was believed to increase desire—and not without some scientific foundation: aniseed contains estrogenic compounds that work up the urges in the same way as female hormones.

Appetizing Stuff
There are several spirits flavored with anise, especially in Mediterranean countries—Greek ouzo, for example—which are drunk to sharpen the appetite. What kind of appetite is often not specified.

You wouldn't think that a plant commonly known as "bird's foot" would do much for your performance in the bedroom, but you'd be wrong. Fenugreek, to give it its more usual name, has aromatic seeds that contain diosgenin, a substance that spices up the hormones and regenerates the generative organs.

117 Brought To Head By Basil

Boccaccio's collection of Italian stories, the *Decameron*, includes an oft-told tale of a pot of basil as a symbol of undying love, a metaphor for the libido-enhancing power the herb is believed to have. The scent is reputed to be irresistible to men, and when used in food increases circulation, relaxes tension, and prolongs lovemaking.

A Herbal High

Voodoo rituals can be pretty wild affairs, and often reach an ecstatic climax. So, the fact basil is used in love ceremonies in Haiti says a lot for the innocent-looking herb's aphrodisiac power.

A sprig of rosemary gives a delicious tang to roast or barbecued meats, but it also helps to enliven the pleasures of the flesh. It's an invigorating herb, promoting vitality, and increases the sensitivity of the skin. If you're not keen on the taste, try putting some in your bathwater instead.

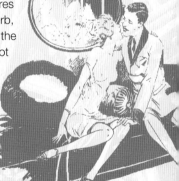

There are many varieties of sage, the principal one used in cooking being blue sage, which in the past has been used as a—sadly ineffective—cure for venereal diseases. However, red sage is the most highly favored among lovers, as, like many herbs, it can both calm anxieties and increase the sex drive.

Just His Cup Of Tea

Around a thousand years ago, the Persian physician and scholar Avicenna wrote about the soothingly seductive power of sage. He is said to have drunk tea made from red sage before going to bed every night, as a "tonic for the nerves." Yeah, right. We believe you.

Thyme grows abundantly in Greece, and it is from the Greek word *thymon*, meaning "courage," that it gets its name—and probably its reputation, too. Faint heart never won fair lady, it's said, and thyme could just stiffen a guy's resolve.

An essential ingredient in much Indian cuisine, cardamom is renowned throughout the subcontinent as a marital aid. It's rich in cineole, which helps blood flow to where it's needed most, and some say that it can help men who have a tendency to reach their peak a little early.

A Breath Of Fresh Air
For anybody hoping to get up close and personal after a spicy, garlicky meal, cardamom has a valuable side effect—sucking or chewing on the seedpods freshens the breath better than a mint.

Cumin seeds, sometimes ground to a powder, give North African dishes their distinctive flavor, but that's not the only reason they're used—the Arabs think stirring it into their food stirs up the loins as well. Europeans tend to be more demure about that sort of thing, and to them cumin is traditionally a symbol of love and fidelity.

A Rose By Any Other Name

Lovers the world over try to win hearts with gifts of roses, but not many know they could perhaps do better feeding them to their dates. The fragrant petals are perfectly edible and added to salads and desserts are said to have magical powers of seduction.

Makes Your Mouth Water
Rosewater, made from boiled-down rose petals, is also believed to cast a tantalizing spell on anyone who consumes it, which accounts for its popularity for flavoring sweet dishes, such as loukoum, or Turkish Delight, in Middle-Eastern and Indian cookery.

The spice mixture known as *ras al-hanout* is widely used in North Africa, as much for its power to arouse as its taste. Essentially a combination of tried and tested aphrodisiacs—cloves, cinnamon, and black pepper—to which Tunisians often add dried rosebuds, it can sometimes be spiked with Spanish Fly *(see page 237)* so watch out!

Capers were originally thought of as an aphrodisiac because the berries resemble testicles, but, being high in antioxidants, eating them will help maintain a healthy sex life. With their rather astringent taste, the unopened flower buds are used to put zest in sauces and garnishes, and the ripe berries as a spicy alternative for olives.

Traditionally served as a sauce to accompany roast lamb or as the flavoring for chewing gum, mint can also be used to compelling effect in all sorts of recipes. It freshens the palate and refreshes the body, and its relaxing properties help to break down inhibitions.

Mint For One Another

Mint's reputation for arousal probably stems from Greek mythology. Pluto fell in love with a nymph called Mente, bewitched by her irresistible scent. When his wife got wind of this, she turned the poor girl into a leafy plant, mint, which still gave off the same alluring aroma.

The Age Of Love

Although it's sometimes known as "love parsley," lovage is not named for its propensity for love but as a corruption of the Latin name *levisticum*. However, just about every part of the lovage plant can be used to awaken the desires of your loved one—the leaves can be used as an aphrodisiac herb, the seeds as a peppery spice, the roots to brew a tea, and the stalks boiled as an invigorating vegetable.

Works Like A Charm

Young women in the Czech Republic have such faith in the captivating charm of lovage that to ensure their love won't be unrequited they hang little bags containing the herb around their necks before going out to meet their beaus.

Fennel Frenzy

It's not the feathery fronds of fennel that tickle the fancy so much as the fleshy stalks and the bulbous base, with its distinctive aniseed flavor. Laboratory rats have been observed showing signs of increased sexual activity after eating fennel—you might like to experiment with it yourself.

129 Yankee Doodle Dandelion

Early American settlers learned the culinary uses of the dandelion from the Native Americans, but it may very well have upset their puritan sensibilities. Whether you use young leaves in salads, or brew the roots for tea, dandelion is notorious for its "uplifting" properties.

Incontinent On The Continent

Unfortunately, it isn't just the sexual urges that dandelion gets going—although the effects are felt in the same region. The French name for the plant, *pissenlit*—which survives in some dialects of British English as piss-a-bed—says it all.

Traditional Chinese medicine refers to the herb dong quai as "female ginseng," and recommends its use for whetting women's sexual appetites and lubricating their libidos. Known in the West as "Chinese angelica," it works a treat on men, too, apparently.

Sí, Sí, Señora

Just south of the border,
down Mexico way, they cook
up a storm with the jacubo
cactus. It's a thorny problem
removing all the spines to get
at the flesh inside, but worth
the effort, as the locals say
it makes you bloom at night,
just like the cactus flowers.

While any of the aphrodisiac herbs work perfectly well on their own, in combination they can unleash a mouthwatering fervor. The French, famous for their expertise in both cuisine and *amour*, put together mixtures of herbs, such as *herbes de Provence* and bouquet garni, to ensure you get things together after the meal, too.

Even The Bible Associates Herbs With Love:
"Better is a dinner of herbs where love is, than a stalled ox and hatred therewith." (PROVERBS 17)

One Man's Meat

The Doctrine of Similars *(see Introduction)* applies to meats as well, but here the rule is, if the animal has a name for rampant randiness—having horns helps—then eating it will make you hot, too. And, going one step further, for the most potent aphrodisiac effect, eat the sexual organs of those animals.

Good-time Grill

If you're not sure which meat is most likely to work for you, you could hedge your bets and go for a mixed grill. Something in there's bound to do the trick. Don't overdo it, though—bulging waistlines and soaring cholesterol levels won't help your chances.

It doesn't take a genius to work out why beef is popular with the men. Bulls have everything going for them in that department: sleek, muscular body, sexual prowess, and the ability to service a whole herd of cows. So, tucking into a juicy steak's got to beef up a guy's chances of getting a slice of that kind of action.

Fast-breeder Reactors

No other animal has quite as raunchy a reputation as the rabbit. The randy little creature is practically a synonym for sex. Jealous? Then try a rabbit stew—it'll soon get you going, and going, and going ...

In many parts of the world they prefer goat and ram to the more docile lamb and mutton of European cuisine—not just because it's more highly flavored but to get a bit of the drive and vigor those horny beasts are renowned for.

Horny Little Devils

Goats have been associated with the devil for centuries, probably because of their sinfully wayward ways. And in classical mythology, the satyr—half man, half goat—was thought to be a wicked little devil with a propensity for promiscuity.

137 Giving Head

There's a specialty
of the West Indies
that they say is guaranteed to put
some power into a man's performance.
Known locally as "mannish water" or
even "power water," it's basically a soup
made from a boiled goat's head, spiced
with garlic, scallions, chilies, chocho
fruit, and green bananas.

Because of their attributes of length, strength, and firmness, bones are often used in recipes designed to give a man a helping hand. One recipe from the Middle East said to give an immediate and long-lasting boost is a soup made from the leg bone of a cow or sheep boiled with onions, garlic, thyme, and cayenne.

Boning Up

Bones are a good source of calcium, which may be useful in maintaining a healthy sex life. But they aren't, in the main, the easiest things to eat—better to use them in stocks and soups, or scoop out the marrow where much of the goodness is.

Stag Party

Perhaps it's because of the antlers *(see page 235)*, or more likely that stags are so notorious for their sexual stamina, there's even a name for their mating: rutting. Whatever the reason, venison is the meat to eat if your love life's in a rut or you need to put life back into the man of your life.

The poor old pig gets a pretty bad press, and is popularly thought of as a dirty, greedy beast—but as pork he becomes a slang term for the penis and sex in general. Pork, especially the meat of the wild boar, is every bit as good an aphrodisiac as any other kind—and in the form of ham or prosciutto can be made to look pretty sexy, too.

Hide The Salami

Pork when spiced up and packed into phallic-shaped skins becomes a salami—and the implications are clear. Surprisingly, during World War II, Italian POWs in Britain found that a couple of slices of Spam luncheon meat were enough to reinforce their standing as Latin Lovers.

141 *Reptilian Rhapsody*

We call a guy possessing easy charm with the ladies
a lounge lizard, which gives some idea of what reptiles
have to offer. And, given their sinuous shape and slinky
behavior, it's no wonder crocodiles and all kinds of lizards
are highly thought of as culinary aphrodisiacs.

Kinky Skinky

The skink, a North-African species of lizard, gets a high rating for arousal,
and is mentioned in the *Arabian Nights* as a food "to make the seed
thicker." The ancient Romans preferred it powdered and dissolved in
wine, and in Persia it was served with amber, pearls, opium, and saffron.

Since Adam and Eve were tempted
by the serpent, snakes have been
associated with enticement. Snake
meat is believed to bestow its seductive
charm and extended muscularity on
anyone who eats it, and in some parts
of the world they'll go to great lengths
to get hold of some.

143 | *My Old Cock Sparrow*

Aphrodite, according to legend, praised sparrows for their loving nature, which is probably how they got to be on the menu for ancient Greeks hankering for some postprandial passion. Trouble is, they're tiny, so you've got to eat quite a few to see any results.

A Lick And A Promise
The fifteenth-century classic guide to sex, *The Perfumed Garden*, recommends a dish of sparrow's tongues to lick your loving into shape. But only during the day—at night you should stick to honey and nuts.

When it comes to getting a rise out of your food, the Chinese set great store by bird's-nest soup. And yes, it is—or should be—made with real birds' nests, boiled in stock, sometimes with sugar added. These are collected from caves around Southeast Asia, where a certain kind of swift makes its home out of congealed saliva and fish spawn.

Get Your Leg Over

French is often called the language
of love—and what could be more
French than frogs' legs? They make
a succulent appetizer—tasting a bit like
chicken—and have a real aphrodisiac kick.

Stand To Attention

Confirmation of the potency of frog's legs comes from researchers at Cornell
University, who were investigating an outbreak of priapism in the French
Foreign Legion. The culprit was their diet of frogs' legs, which contained
quantities of canthardin, the active ingredient of Spanish Fly *(see page 237)*.

The Roman writer Martial thought that to get maximum uplift from snails, they should be eaten raw and without any sauce, but most people these days would find that a shortcut to the bathroom, not the bedroom. Better, and probably just as potent, is to have them baked in butter with lashings of garlic and herbs.

You might think that poultry would be for the chicks, but, like most meats, it works its magic mainly on the cock of the species. Alchemists reckoned ducks and geese helped firm things up, if their long sturdy necks are anything to go by— but perhaps capons (castrated roosters) are best avoided.

Young Love

In the Philippines they like their ducks young—very young. The specialty dish *balut* is actually a serving of fertilized duck eggs, or, more accurately, duck embryos, and is much sought after by up-and-coming young Filipinos.

Made from the livers of geese that have been force-fed until they almost burst, pâté de foie gras is the ultimate in decadent foods. Its smooth, creamy, melt-in-the-mouth texture makes it pretty sexy, too, and in France it's almost compulsory as an hors d'oeuvre to a seductive dinner date.

149 | *Who Came First?*

An almost universal symbol of fertility, eggs appear in a large number of aphrodisiac recipes. Because of their association with new life, they are supposed to have rejuvenating powers, but they provide a fair bit of energy, too, and downing a few raw eggs just before sex will improve your staying power.

Egging You On

An artist carving on emu eggs in Australia recently made a startling discovery: the dust from the shells was dramatically increasing his sex drive. Local emu farmers confirmed his findings, saying they looked on emu-egg dust as a natural alternative to Viagra.

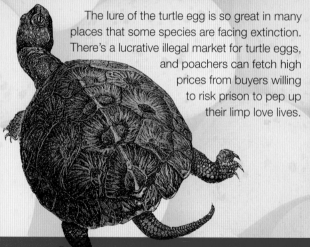

The lure of the turtle egg is so great in many places that some species are facing extinction. There's a lucrative illegal market for turtle eggs, and poachers can fetch high prices from buyers willing to risk prison to pep up their limp love lives.

151 A Cock-And-Bull Story

Now, if the meat of randy beasts can confer its priapic power on the consumer, then eating the genitalia must work even better, right? Well, that's the theory, and there are plenty of people who swear that it works.

No Place For A Lady

A recently opened restaurant in Beijing serves nothing but dishes made from the penises and testicles of various animals, cashing in on the Chinese obsession with sexual prowess. So far, it's been a resounding success, but they're having a bit of trouble attracting female customers.

Unfortunately, the animal most usually thought as symbolizing masculinity in the Orient is the tiger, an endangered species. And guess what cut of meat is most popular—you got it, tiger tool. It's available in the Far East as a meaty main course, in pills and potions, and even pickled in brandy.

Traditional Chinese medicine prescribes the genitals of bull seals for cases of impotence and lack of libido, and this has provoked a roaring trade in seal penises smuggled from Canada. Demand for this delicacy has become enormous, and now outstrips supply, so many traders are substituting genitalia from cattle, and even cats and dogs.

As well as being infamous for his profligate way with the chicks, the rooster is well known as the bird that gets us up in the morning—and don't forget his more earthy name, cock. In medieval Europe, wives dissatisfied with their husbands' limp performance cooked a soup of beans and cocks' testicles in the hope some of that would rub off on them.

Cock-and-ball?

The ancient Roman philosopher Pliny the Elder advised some quite revolting remedies for a flagging desire. He suggested that men should wear parts of a vulture's lung as an amulet. If this was not available, Pliny thought that the right testicle of a cock would do the trick just as well.

155 Battering Ram

The horniest of the
domesticated animals, in every
sense, are goats and rams.
The secret of their success, so
they say, is in their testicles,
which appear regularly
on the dining tables
of lonely goatherds.
Strangely, they're not so
keen on billy's willy or ram's rammer.

After a hard day on the trail, a lonesome cowboy might need a bit of a boost before moseying into town for a night of "howdy pardner." Luckily, he can easily rustle up a dish of Rocky Mountain Oysters to fortify the inner man. The main ingredient? Bulls' balls.

Meat Balls, Italian-style

Bartolomeo Scappi, a sixteenth-century Italian chef, often prepared a pie of seasoned bull's testicles for his employer. While this would normally be guaranteed to provoke a raunchy reaction, in this case, however, it was probably a waste of time—his master was Pope Pius V.

157 The Amber Nectar

You may be convinced by the argument for eating the wedding tackle of prominently potent animals to harness a bit of their power, but some pundits go a bit further—maybe a step too far. The Roman writer Paulinus admitted that bull's penis came up with the goods, but suggested that drinking bull's urine would be just as effective.

There's some dispute over the efficacy of whale meat as an aphrodisiac, but it's nevertheless still sought after in Japan. The most highly prized dish for the aspiring studs there is made from the penis of the minke whale. Presumably they then have a "whale of a time."

Come Again?

The sperm whale's reputation for being a love food is, unfortunately, based on a misunderstanding. It gets its name not from its sexual prowess but because whalers thought the waxy fluid spermaceti found in its head resembled semen.

159 Feelgood Factor

Candies and desserts are more associated with love and romance than sex and fertility, but shouldn't be dismissed as a tool in the armory of *amour*. Generally speaking, they make you feel comfortable and relaxed and lower your inhibitions, putting you in the mood for love.

Meats Are From Mars, Sweets Are From Venus

Most people think of aphrodisiacs as having a physiological effect—mostly on males—boosting libido, intensifying and prolonging lovemaking, and generally fortifying the sexual organs. But there are also those that work on the psyche, increasing desire and making you more receptive.

Montezuma II, the Aztec emperor, is said to have drunk up to fifty cups of chocolate a day in order to whip up sufficient ardor to serve his harem of 600 ladies. Another randy chocoholic, the ubiquitous Marquis de Sade, wrote to his wife during one of his many sojourns in jail: "I wish for a chocolate cake so dense that it is black, like the devil's ass is blackened by smoke."

Chock Horror!

Chocolate's reputation as an aphrodisiac is supported by the fact that it contains phenylethylamine, the same amphetamine that courses through our veins when in love.

161 M– M– Mmmm ... That's Nice

Nobody knows how the rumor started, but sometime in the 1970s word got round that the green food coloring in some candies had aphrodisiac properties. Top of the list of sexy sweeties were green M&Ms, which young men were picking out of the packs to tempt their dates. Less popular, but reportedly just as effective, were green jellybeans and Gummi Bears.

Add a few extra erotic ingredients to a chocolate bar—peanuts or coconut, for example—elongate it slightly, and you've got a seductive and suggestive treat. Take a look at the commercials for some of these sweet snacks, and you'll see how the connotations are exploited by the ad-men.

A Box Full Of Chox

An apocryphal story doing the rounds in the 1960s told how a well-known British rock star and his then girlfriend used a Mars bar—a dubiously phallic chocolate bar, whose advertising slogan was, "A Mars a day helps you work, rest, and play"—as a dildo. Needless to say, sales soared.

163 Easy Come, Easy Go

Herbalists in China and India have long been recommending licorice to turn on the love juices, especially in women. Chewing on the sweet roots of the plant even gets mentioned in the *Kama Sutra* as a recipe for arousal. Best not to OD on the stuff, however—it's also a powerful laxative.

Whatever Turns You On
A study by the Smell & Taste Treatment and Research Foundation, Chicago, found that the scent of black licorice increases blood flow to the penis, and more so when combined with the aroma of doughnuts. It is also sexually arousing to women, especially if enhanced by the smell of cucumber.

You can get it firm or soft, thick or thin, but honey in all its varieties is packed with goodies to get you going, and sweetness to help you keep it up. More than 2,000 years ago, Hippocrates recommended it as an invigorating elixir for lovers, but it had been used to inspire love and lust for centuries before that.

165 Never On A Sundae

You might have thought that ice cream was likely to cool your ardor, but it actually has much the same effect as other sweets in putting lovers in the mood. It's also usually flavored with vanilla, chocolate, or fruits, whose amatory effects are legendary. Don't forget to put a cherry on top.

Cold Comfort
If the idea of ice cream leaves you cold, consider turning up the heat with a baked Alaska—ice cream on a flan base, totally covered in egg whites whipped with sugar, cooked in a hot oven until the meringue is crisp. The ice cream will still be firm and cold, but it could melt your lover's heart.

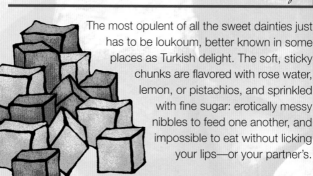

The most opulent of all the sweet dainties just has to be loukoum, better known in some places as Turkish delight. The soft, sticky chunks are flavored with rose water, lemon, or pistachios, and sprinkled with fine sugar: erotically messy nibbles to feed one another, and impossible to eat without licking your lips—or your partner's.

Land Of Milk And Honey

Milk and cream, especially when whipped and served on fruity desserts, is reminiscent of the juices it is said to provoke. In India, camel's milk in particular is thought to nourish the nether regions, and *The Perfumed Garden* recommends it mixed with honey for men past their prime.

To round off a meal before retiring to the bedroom, what could be better than cheese? It contains more phenylethylamine—which gives the same buzz as making love—than chocolate, and a fatty acid similar to female pheromones *(see page 330)*. Perhaps that's why in Italy they say that a good cheese tastes like the scent of a woman.

Blue Heaven

The legendary lover Casanova relied on a number of foods to have his way with the ladies. A favorite of his was blue cheese washed down with dark red wine, which he said could "restore an old love and ripen a young one."

169 | *Melting Like Butter*

When cream is churned to form butter, it becomes more than just an aphrodisiac—it's an essential partner to many other erotic foods. Used in cooking, it adds a sexy richness to everything from starters to desserts, and as a garnish—well, can you imagine eating asparagus or corn on the cob without it?

Buttering Up

It has to be mentioned, I'm afraid, that butter can also be used externally when things are not going smoothly for a couple. If you've any doubts about its efficacy, go see the movie *Last Tango in Paris*.

♥178   Foods To Raise The Dead

Many fruits and seeds are pressed to produce oils for culinary use, but none is as sumptuous and seductive as olive oil. It retains all the stimulating goodness of the olive (*see page 35*), helps keep a healthy blood flow, and can be sensually drizzled on all kinds of foods to give them a glistening, lubricious sheen.

If you believe the rhyme about what little girls are made of, the Moroccan dessert *majoon* must be the essence of femininity. It is made from powdered hemp, honey, dried fruits, nuts, and spices—usually cinnamon and nutmeg—which should make the girls more girly and the boys, well, more eager.

Frogs And Snails And Puppydogs' Tails

Some Moroccans feel that *majoon* is just too feminine, and needs a bit of a macho kick, so they add a renowned male arouser, too—powdered lizard. You have been warned.

A really sweet sweet found all over the Middle East, halva is made from tahini—a paste of ground roasted sesame seeds and boiled sugar or honey, often dotted with fruits and nuts. A real energizer, it gives a sugar rush to the libido.

Intercourse

Water ices—or sorbets—have all the feelgood properties of ice cream, but, as they're made without dairy products or eggs—they are lighter and more refreshing. Often served between the courses of a meal, they help to cleanse the palate and stimulate the appetite—in more ways than one.

Nuts—which have been prized for their aphrodisiac qualities for thousands of years—can be chopped or flaked and sprinkled on all kinds of sweets and desserts to give them a more crunchy texture. And, who knows, it might perhaps encourage some more interesting and intimate nibbling ...

The Shape Of Things To Come?

Marzipan, sweetened almond paste, is sometimes available as little sweets in the shape of various fruits. You could make some for yourself to serve as the climax of a seductive dinner—but why stick to fruit shapes? Let your imagination run wild ...

Sweetmeats

One very exotic dessert—or is it a main course?—is described in the *Kama Sutra* as being a guaranteed passion provoker. Take one or two ram's or goat's testicles and boil in milk—camel's, if you've got it—which has been sweetened with honey. Serve, then wait for the desire to kick in.

In the Middle East they don't take any chances when it comes to seduction— one aphrodisiac might not do the trick on its own, so put a few together just to make sure. For example, there's a pudding made with hedge-sparrow eggs and rice cooked in butter and honey, which, with all those powerful ingredients combined, is said to be a surefire winner.

Custard's Last Stand

Custard makes an arousing alternative to cream for topping desserts or even eating on its own as a crème brûlée or flan. The recipe consists of eggs, milk, and sugar flavored with vanilla—all tried-and-tested erotic ingredients.

Many aphrodisiacs are believed to work even better when combined, and sometimes this throws up some weird and wonderful partnerships with surprisingly satisfying results. Try serving dark chocolate with a glass of red wine instead of dessert—wine and chocolate have similarly stimulating qualities —or a dish of strawberries with a good claret.

Tipsy Tips

A good way of enhancing the erotic effect of alcohol is to use it as an ingredient in desserts. Fruits marinaded in spirits, served with a little cream or ice cream, are always tempting, or you could lace a favorite dessert with brandy to give it a shot of sexy power.

A date doesn't always mean a romantic dinner, and sometimes you need a quick-and-easy snack to prepare you for the evening's activities. A simple peanut butter-and-jelly sandwich is ideal for providing the necessary sexual energy, and if things are going well, forget the bread—spread soft peanut butter on each other and lick it off.

179 Doing The Splits

The banana split is possibly the rudest-looking dessert there is. Depending on how you present it, a banana can be provocatively phallic if served whole with a couple of scoops of ice cream, and drizzled with chocolate sauce and a squirt of whipped cream, or tantalizingly female if split lengthwise and arranged in a manner suggestive of the labia, then decorated with whipped cream and a strategically placed cherry.

It Ain't What You Do, It's The Way That You Do It

Presentation is all important, especially when it comes to desserts. Use your imagination and creative flair to make your sweets into suggestive shapes that will tempt your lover to an orgy of erotic eating.

One dictionary defines the chocolate éclair as "a baker's confection long in shape, and short in duration," which is an accurate description of this orgasmic cake filled with custard or cream and covered in chocolate. Let's hope it doesn't have the same effect on your lovemaking.

A Stiff Drink

According to the humorist Ogden Nash, "Candy is dandy, but liquor is quicker," and he may have a point. All kinds of drinks are thought to be more arousing than aphrodisiac foods. A few are nonalcoholic but alcohol is the active ingredient in the majority. Whichever you choose, the dosage is vital—in the right quantities it may unleash the libido; too much and your evening could end up as a downer.

Bedtime Beverage

First on the list of drinks to fortify a flagging libido has to be hot chocolate, despite its reputation as an antidote to insomnia. The Aztecs, who first used chocolate to arouse the passions, took it in liquid form, and the modern equivalent, in the shape of a hot drink made with milk, is a sumptuous way both to relax and to fuel the fires of desire.

Sleeping Partners
Generally speaking, although milk is said to increase the sex drive, hot milky drinks other than chocolate should be avoided. Their soporific effects make it an ideal nightcap, but only if you're planning a good night's sleep.

Caffeine, like alcohol, figures prominently in drinks designed to get things going. Coffee is renowned for its invigorating effect on both mind and body, and can give a wake-up call to the libido, too. A small cup of good strong coffee could be just the thing to counteract lethargy after a heavy meal.

Tea contains caffeine, too, along with antioxidants, which are thought to be necessary for a healthy love life. In countries such as India and China where tea is grown—and in Britain where it has become the national drink—they prefer it to coffee as a warm-up for hot-blooded action.

Inflaming Infusions

Other so-called "teas" come highly recommended for would-be lovers, especially in the Ayurvedic traditions of India. These are actually infusions of herbs or spices, such as cinnamon or nutmeg, which are known for their erotic properties in liquid form.

One way to get all the energizing goodness of aphrodisiac fruits is to squeeze it out of them. Fruit juices of all kinds are refreshing and invigorating, and are a good alternative to alcoholic drinks as aperitifs, or if you're in the bar and want to keep your wits about you—in case things get serious.

185 Hitting The "C" Spot

You can inject a caffeine shot into your lovemaking even if you don't like hot drinks. Fizzy drinks such as Coke and Pepsi contain enough to keep you going, and there are even some that deliver more of a hit than coffee. They make good mixers, too, enhancing the erotic power of alcohol—and maybe counteracting some of its depressant effect.

Amorous Athletics
Athletes have found that a shot of a glucose or a hydrating drink can improve their performance, and there's no reason to doubt that these "sports drinks" will work away from the track and field, too. If it's stamina and energy you're after, you might want to give them a try.

Not yet readily available in the West, but increasingly popular in Southeast Asia, snake blood is reportedly better than most other aphrodisiac drinks. Parlors in Malaysia now provide facilities where men lie on the floor and suck the pierced tail of a live rattlesnake to revitalize their love lives.

No Worries

It's thought that oat straw helps to keep the nervous system in balance and calm anxieties. If you're worried about your amorous abilities, try a decoction of an ounce of oat straw boiled in a pint of water for twenty minutes—apparently it improves the sex drive, too.

Another powerful brew for stimulating the libido can be made by grinding together equal parts of licorice root, sesame seeds, and fennel seeds and infusing them in boiling water. Strain the liquor into a glass and leave to cool, and drink just before making love for maximum effect.

Herbal High

These days, there are more and more herbal teas appearing in health-food stores for people trying to cut down on caffeine. Many of them are blends of herbs with ginseng—a potent ardor arouser—which could have the opposite of the relaxing effect you might expect.

I Put A Spell On You

Herbal teas aren't just for improving your sexual performance. The Celtic druids, for instance, believed that some decoctions were magical love potions. A tea made with rosemary, thyme, nutmeg, mint, rose petals, and honey was thought to make you irresistible—but only if brewed on a Friday during a waxing moon, and then served the following Friday to the object of your desires.

That Old Black Magic

When making magical potions, the ceremony can be important for them to work. The druids' love potion should be mixed while reciting this rhyme: *By light of moon waxing, I brew this tea / To make [name] desire me. / Goddess of Love hear now my plea, / Let [name] desire me. / So mote it be.*

An eighteenth-century book on herbs contains the following recipe for a steamy stimulant: "Into a steaming-hot cup of very strong coffee or hot chocolate place a small quantity of crushed nutmeg and two whole juniper berries. Let the mixture stand for two minutes and then, on the surface of the beverage, sprinkle a bit of cinnamon." Hot stuff, and bound to ignite the libido.

191 The Hard Stuff

The main reason that alcohol is associated with seduction is that, rather than raising levels of desire, it lowers the levels of inhibition. A few glasses of your favorite tipple will give you the Dutch courage to make the moves—or weaken your ability to resist them—but more than that and you're likely to be unable to come up with the goods.

What A Performance
In *The Marriage of Figaro*, the playwright Beaumarchais ponders the nature of man: "Drinking when we are not thirsty, and making love all year round, madam: that is all there is to distinguish us from other animals. The former characteristic undoubtedly inspires the latter."

In Vino Veritas

Dionysus—and his Roman incarnation, Bacchus—the classical god of wine, is often portrayed as the instigator of wild orgies, presumably as a result of the drinks he promoted. There's no doubt that wine is a very sexy drink and an essential accompaniment to a romantic dinner. As well as the alcohol, red wine contains antioxidants that might make your heart beat a little quicker.

193 The Real Thing

From toasting a wedding to launching a ship, champagne is the wine of celebration, and it adds sparkle to any special occasion. It's a tempting tool of seduction for any time of the day, and popping a bottle of bubbly quickly gets you into an amiable mood, as the fizz helps the alcohol get into the bloodstream more quickly.

Three's Company
Edward FitzGerald, the translator of the Persian *Rubáiyát of Omar Khayyám*, knew what he was talking about when he said, "A jug of wine, a loaf of bread—and thou."

For a long time, absinthe was banned in many countries because of its supposed mind-altering effects—and the legal situation is still somewhat cloudy in the USA—but it's recently been making a comeback. This bright-green aniseed-flavored drink spiked with wormwood looks and smells as erotic and exotic as it tastes, spicing up the sex life and conjuring up images of the seamier side of Parisian nightlife at the end of the nineteenth century.

195 *A Happy Mead-yum!*

The Vikings were a macho crew, renowned for their carousing and wenching, and it's from their custom of serving mead—made from fermented honey—to newlyweds that we get the word "honeymoon." The young couples drank mead for the first month of their marriage to sweeten the relationship and give them the necessary stamina for a happy married life.

Of all the different kinds of beer, rich, dark stout is possibly the most likely to give your sex life a boost. To add to this, one brewer in Ireland apparently makes a stout containing extract of oysters, but, even so, it's unlikely to replace champagne as the flirt's drink of choice.

Strange Brew

The ancient Egyptians looked on beer as a divine drink. Nowadays, it doesn't have quite the same cachet—alhough some say that a couple of glasses makes them feel amorous. Beware the side effects, though; beer's a diuretic that can get the wrong juices flowing and the fizz can give you gas.

197 For Goodness Sake

In Japan, rice is considered a symbol of fertility. Sake, a rice wine, is frequently drunk as a stimulating part of Japanese wedding ceremonies. Even so, you should try not to say "Chin chin" when imbibing in Japan—this expression refers to the male genitals.

A Stiff Drink

Alcohol comes in its strongest concentration in spirits such as brandy and whiskey, so they are considered by some to be the most powerful defense-lowering drinks. Many of them are distilled from aphrodisiac fruits or grains, reinforcing the idea that after a meal they will aid the move from dining table to couch.

Hot Or On The Rocks?

Sake is often served hot, in small cups especially designed for the purpose. Some of these have erotic pictures painted inside that can be seen when the cup is filled with the clear sake. In contrast, in the West spirits are usually taken cold, even iced. Let's hope it's only the drink that's "on the rocks."

Sweet And Lowdown

The after-dinner digestif is a sexy
way to round off a meal for two,
and more often than not it's going
to be a sweet liqueur that will warm
you through and put you in a mellow
mood. These syrupy seducers are
usually flavored with fruits or herbs
to stimulate, too, so don't worry that
you'll be too drowsy to make the moves.

Monkey Business
Some of the best known of the lusty liqueurs—such as green
Chartreuse and Benedictine—rely on a subtle blend of sensuous
herbs for their erotic properties. Strangely, the creative herbalists
behind these devilish drinks were celibate monks.

Maybe it's the shape of the cactus from which it's distilled, or perhaps from the worm, traditionally happily pickled in the bottom the bottle, but whatever it is, tequila is considered as potent sexually as it is in degrees proof, and has been used to break down inhibitions for generations down Mexico way.

Mexican Magic

The damiana herb, a renowned aphrodisiac (*see page 249*), grows wild in parts of Mexico, and it is used as the basis for a liqueur that packs quite a poke. It can be drunk on its own or in place of tequila in a margarita—in fact, locals say that the first margarita was made using damiana liqueur.

If You've Got The Bottle

Damiana liqueur is sold in a bottle that reinforces its erotic reputation. It's in the shape of a voluptuously well-endowed Incan fertility goddess, whose charms are not left to the imagination.

Damiana also features in a long drink known as damiana tincture, but it needs a bit of forward planning. Soak damiana leaves in a pint of vodka or rum for five days, then strain off the liquor and put it to one side. Soak the same leaves in a pint of water for a further five days. Warm the water infusion and sweeten with honey, then add the alcohol to it. Drinking a couple of glasses before bed is recommended.

203 Dominican Spiced Punch

The Dominican Republic has its own version of spiced wine or punch, known as Mama Juana. The main ingredients are rum, red wine, and honey, with a mixture of herbs and tree barks left to steep in the bottle. It's sold locally as an aphrodisiac rather than a drink, and most people prefer to make their own at home.

Popular at Christmas time, in the northern hemisphere at least, mulled wine warms the heart and gives friends—and lovers—a feelgood glow. Red wine, sometimes fortified with a spirit such as brandy, is warmed gently with a mix of spices—typically cloves, cinnamon, nutmeg, and lemon zest—that give it its passionate punch.

Frigga's Fruit

At the same time as the mulled wine, we also have mistletoe. Although not edible, the tradition of kissing under the mistletoe might just get the ball rolling. The parasitic plant was considered to be a powerful sexual symbol by the Vikings, and associated with Frigga, the goddess of love.

Getting It Together

Never mix your drinks, so they say, but that would mean missing out on a whole bunch of great little lust inducers. There are far too many cocktails to give a comprehensive list here, and nearly all claim to assist in the art of seduction. From the classic Dry Martini to the Slow Comfortable Screw Against The Wall—really, I kid you not—the choice is yours.

A Sting In The Tail
It's not just the mixture of drinks in the glass that make a cocktail into a sophisticated seducer's favorite tipple. It has to be served in the correct glass, sometimes frosted with sugar and garnished with an appropriate fruit—a slice of orange or lemon, or a sexy cherry, or an olive on a stick.

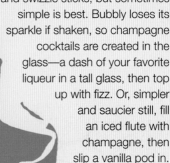

Cocktails often have fantastically complex recipes involving special equipment like shakers, ice crushers, and swizzle sticks, but sometimes simple is best. Bubbly loses its sparkle if shaken, so champagne cocktails are created in the glass—a dash of your favorite liqueur in a tall glass, then top up with fizz. Or, simpler and saucier still, fill an iced flute with champagne, then slip a vanilla pod in.

207 *A Gland In The Hand*

If you can't face the thought of real monkey glands *(see page 239)*, there's a Monkey Gland cocktail that's said to have much the same effect: two parts gin, one part fresh orange juice, a dash of absinthe, and a dash of grenadine. It's a meaty mouthful—but it's suitable for vegetarians, too.

To get a party going with a real swing, have a bowl of Orgasmic Punch on hand. In a large bowl, mix together two bottles of white rum, three or four bottles of white wine, a cup of triple sec, the juice of ten oranges and six lemons, then add a cup of sugar, a couple of ounces each of damiana tincture and muira puama tincture, pineapple chunks, and a few split vanilla pods. Stir well, and float some clove-studded oranges and rose petals on top. Don't be surprised if some couples leave early.

Packing A Punch

While cocktails are normally mixed in small quantities, enough for a couple of glasses at most, punch is more of a party animal. It's usually a wine-based concoction with fruit, and is prepared and served in a punch bowl with plenty for everyone.

Smooth Operator

If you're worried that alcohol could stop you raising the necessary enthusiasm for your amorous plans, opt for one of the teetotal alternatives, such as a Vanilla Aphrodisiac Smoothie. Heat—but don't boil!—a cup of milk with 15 cloves, 15 cardamom seeds, two cinnamon sticks, and a couple of split vanilla pods, then strain and refrigerate. When chilled, blend with a cup of frozen vanilla yogurt and honey. Just as provocative, but without the risk of letting you down at a crucial moment.

No Hang-ups, No Hangover

There's no end of exciting cocktails that don't involve booze, from fruit juice combinations to the Virgin Mary—Bloody Mary without the vodka. The great thing is that you can drink these all evening and still carry on all night.

Napoleon's frustrated lover got so fed up with hearing,
"Not tonight, Josephine," that she served him a
chocolate-and-coffee drink spiced with lavender flowers,
in the hope that it would revive the battle-weary general.
It apparently brought the soldier to attention, and soon
became his favorite nighttime drink.

211 *Mexican Mover*

Some think that if a margarita doesn't do it for you, then nothing will, especially if damiana liqueur is used instead of the French component. In its classic form, it's equal parts of tequila, Triple Sec or Cointreau, and lime juice—although the ratios vary from bar to bar—all garnished with a generous slice of lime. It should be served in a glass the rim of which has been wetted with the slice of lime then dipped in salt.

Fresh As A Daisy

Margarita means "daisy," and comes from the Latin for pearl—which itself has aphrodisiac associations *(see page 236)*. The drink's origins are shrouded in mystery—one story is that it was invented in 1938 at a bar in Tijuana, Mexico, for the actress Marjorie (Margarita in Spanish) King.

Vanilla Tincture is an after-dinner digestif to settle the stomach but get pulses racing. Split two or three vanilla pods and drop them whole into a bottle of brandy. Leave the vanilla to infuse for at least two weeks, then serve in warmed brandy balloons, preferably on a deep sofa beside an open fire.

| *Try Martini*

Gin is not everybody's cup of tea, and it got a bad press in the eighteenth and nineteenth centuries as it was the booze of choice of London's streetwalkers at the time. True, it is still sometimes known as "Mother's ruin," but don't let that put you off some of the gin-based cocktails: a Dry Martini—gin and vermouth—might help break the ice at the bar. Shaken or stirred, it might also lubricate the libido.

Her Wit's End
The writer and wit Dorothy Parker wasn't averse to a Dry Martini or three, but generally knew when to stop, if only for appearances' sake. After one cocktail party she was overheard saying, "One more drink and I'd have been under the host."

A couple of cocktail recipes include rose syrup to give a romantic touch to what might otherwise seem weapons of conquest. Rose Martini, for example, is vodka, Cointreau, cranberry juice, and rose syrup; and Eden is an even more potent mixture of gin, Campari, lemon juice, and rose syrup served on the rocks. Each should be garnished with a few rose petals.

215 | *Kisses Much Sweeter Than Wine*

A sweet little cocktail for sweethearts, the French Kiss combines the provocative powers of alcohol, chocolate, and cream. Mix together two shots of vodka, one and a half shots of Chambord (raspberry liqueur), a shot of Godiva white-chocolate liqueur, and a helping of heavy cream. Serve chilled, garnished with a chocolate kiss.

Drinks manufacturers are constantly coming up with new ideas to lead us into temptation, but the new ones are seldom better than the old favorites. An exception, however, are the blends of spirits and cream—sumptuous, sophisticated, and seductive.

An All-Rounder

"Only Irish coffee provides in a single glass all four essential food groups: alcohol, caffeine, sugar, and fat." ALEX LEVINE, HUMORIST

Lotions
And Potions

You might think that there are enough aphrodisiac foods and drinks to satisfy the most demanding lovers, but in the quest for the definitive answer to a maiden's prayers, lovers have often turned to more drastic measures. These include magic potions, herbal preparations, and drugs both medicinal and "recreational." You'll find a pharmacopeia of remedies here—everything from Spanish Fly to Viagra.

217 *Something For The Wife*

Traditional remedies for flagging libido or wilting virility are passed down from lustful generation to generation, and are often dismissed as being old wives' tales. But, hey, maybe some of the old wives knew a thing or two about keeping their old men interested. If your local folklore has a recipe for hotting things up, try it—there's no smoke without fire.

Back in the Middle Ages, Bishop Burchard I of Worms in Germany noticed the locals making what they called "love bread." The womenfolk danced naked in the wheat, which was then ground counterclockwise to make flour. Bread made from this was believed to make the woman who served it absolutely irresistible to her man.

A Myth Is As Good As A Mile

Legends surrounding the ingredients of love potions link them to the sexual exploits of gods and mythical creatures, and invest them with the same mystical powers. Those stories had to start somewhere, and it often turns out that there is some scientific foundation for the claims, too.

Come Blow On Your Horn

Because of its priapic appearance, rhino horn has been prized for bolstering male members since time immemorial. The fibrous protuberance is ground to a powder to make it easier to swallow; it contains calcium and phosphorus, which could help increase sexual stamina—but only in very large doses.

It's a bit tricky to get hold of, outside fairy tales, but unicorn horn is believed to be even more effective than rhino horn in revitalizing the virility. If you do manage to come across one of these mythical creatures, check its gender before hunting it down—apparently only male horns will do.

The Tooth, The Whole Tooth, And Nothing But The Tooth

When whalers first pulled narwhals out of the sea, they thought they'd found marine unicorns, as this whale has a long, single tusk. The rumor soon got about, and the poor animals were hunted not only for their meat and oil, but for the ersatz "unicorn horn," too.

Boning Up

When tigers were more common than they are today, Asian men concerned about their masculine maintenance resorted to preparations of ground tiger bones. Alas, the supply was no more sustainable than their drooping manhood, and the noble creatures have been hunted almost to extinction.

To tell the truth, most animal horns and bones are pretty indigestible. Perhaps that's why the Chinese came up with an alternative way of extracting their bracing properties: velvet from deer antlers. The velvety covering of antlers rubs off easily and can be brewed into potions or dried and formed into pills—which now fetch high prices all over the world.

Stick At It

Aristotle was one of the first to notice that the penises of dogs and wolves contain a bony structure called a baculum, or "little stick." It turned out that many other animals have this handy tool, and the story must have got around that eating bones and horns could get humans one, too.

223 *Wisdom Of Pearls*

Cleopatra had a fairly hectic social life, by all accounts, and she put her success with the guys down to pearls dissolved in wine—or possibly vinegar, but then ancient Egyptian wine probably wasn't of the finest quality. The theory was that pearls, just like Aphrodite, came out of oyster shells, so they just had to be aphrodisiacs.

In 1772, the Marquis de Sade fed Spanish Fly to a group of prostitutes in an attempt to stimulate orgiastic behavior. But, far from getting the Marquis laid, this dangerous substance laid the prostitutes low. When he was tried and found guilty of poisoning, De Sade was forced to flee France, no longer being considered an upright citizen.

Beetle Mania

Spanish Fly is not in fact a fly but a green blister beetle, *Cantharis vesicatoria*. Since Roman times it has earned an undeserved reputation as an aphrodisiac because it causes swelling of the organs. However, it is more likely to lower a corpse than raise a member, since the effects can be fatal.

225 *Nothing But A Hound Dog*

The ancient Egyptians revered the jackal as a god, and his reputation held good until the Middle Ages in Europe. He was thought to be a raunchy beast, and for some reason jackal bile got a name as a sexual stimulant for both men and women. But don't go eating any of that stuff—it's meant to be applied externally to the genitals.

Dr. Serge Vonoroff, a Russian medic working in France in the 1920s, suggested that implanting bits of monkey testicle into a human scrotum would enhance a man's prowess—he had probably misunderstood the Asian folklore that monkey's pituitary glands had aphrodisiac powers. All the same, he started the ball rolling, so to speak, and monkey glands of all sorts now appear in impotence remedies.

The Steaks Are High

Monkey glands' efficacy is well known but not everybody can face actually swallowing them. For the squeamish, there is a Monkey Gland cocktail *(see page 218)*, and in South Africa a Monkey Gland steak—actually a beefsteak marinated in vinegar, mustard, tomatoes, and Worcestershire sauce.

227 The Toad To Ruin

Although primarily taken for their psychedelic effect, extracts of toad venom—known as "stone"—were found to induce erotic reactions, too. Users reported increased feelings of sexual desire and arousal, prompting a spate of "toad licking" in those parts of the USA where the poisonous species *Bufo bufo gargarizans*, *Bufo vulgaris*, and *Bufo marinus* could be tracked down.

It's not just frogs' legs that inflame the erogenous zones (*see page 154*), their saliva is believed to bring on similar symptoms, too. Frog spit is also reputed to have antiseptic, anesthetic, and even narcotic properties, so is much used in alternative medicine.

Some Day My Prince Will Come

The mind-altering and aphrodisiac qualities of some amphibians' bodily fluids may be at the root of a well-known fairy story—the one where the princess kisses the frog and it turns into a handsome prince. The poor girl was probably the victim of both hallucination and wishful thinking.

Help With The Hump

Camels, not
surprisingly, have
a central place in
the pharmacology
of traditional Middle-
Eastern folk medicine.
Their milk is thought
to increase the sex
drive (*see page 176*), and
rendered camel hump, when
smeared on the affected parts, is
believed to give a lift to couples
with penetrating problems.

We're moving into the realms of unpleasantness here, but in many different parts of the world cockroaches are considered not only edible but aphrodisiac, too. One recipe for sexual success is to add dried and ground cockroach, mixed with cinnamon, to a cup of coffee. It's not yet available in your local Starbucks, though.

Love Bugs

In the West, we tend to dislike insects, especially in the kitchen or medicine cupboard, but elsewhere they are often considered to have erotic powers. Ants figure on the menu in many places—if you're looking for something to give your love life a lift, try them covered in chocolate, or in olive oil.

To The Manure Born

Leeches are apparently making a comeback in modern medicine, but not yet in the way they were used in medieval Europe. A popular remedy for drooping desire in those days was an ointment concocted from dead leeches left to rot in a stinking dungheap.

The idea of eating part of an animal to absorb some of its promiscuous prowess can go a step too far. Several cultures have suggested eating human genitals to improve performance, and eunuchs in China would eat the brains of executed criminals in the hope of restoring their missing manhood.

Come For A Meal

Desperately seeking a libido boost, hopeful lovers have ingested mixtures of—among other things—menstrual blood, placenta, and, of course, semen. One particularly unpleasant ancient Roman remedy was pellets made from the sperm of virile young men mixed with hawk or eagle excrement.

233 *Garden Of Delights*

Herbs have been used medicinally for thousands of years in every culture, and the majority of the world's population still rely on herbalism for their health—even modern Western pharmacology uses plant extracts. There are herbal remedies for just about every ill, including a whole bunch of treatments for achieving a healthy love life.

According to the Greek philosopher Theophrastus, the herb known then as satyrion—probably a kind of ragwort—could bolster a man's sexual stamina enough for him to make love seventy times in a row. Probably an exaggeration of the plant's potency, but it became so popular that the supply eventually became exhausted—not the only thing, by the sound of it.

Legendary Lechers

Satyrion took its name from the mythical satyrs—half man, half goat—that accompanied the god Dionysus. They are frequently shown in classical art with prominent erections, and had legendary appetites for wine, women, and any pleasure of the flesh.

235 Barking Up The Right Tree

Yohimbine comes from the bark of the yohimbe tree, a native of West Africa, where it is traditionally used in marriage and fertility ceremonies. It can have a mildly hallucinogenic effect when smoked, and has been used as a local anesthetic, but its main claim to fame is the way it dilates blood vessels, increasing the flow where it's needed most for conjugal bliss.

The leaves and heads of the damiana plant are used widely in South America to reawaken the enthusiasm of lackluster lovers *(see page 212)*. Damiana contains phytestrogens, which mimic the female hormones and crank up the libido in both sexes. Now available in tablet form, it was originally mixed into the food at mealtimes—three or four times a day if necessary.

Getting Hold Of Things

Some exotic fresh herbs aren't obtainable outside their country of origin, and many can only be found in specialist herbalist shops. But the good news is that more and more aphrodisiac herbs are being processed into pills and capsules, and sold in alternative-medicine shops and on the Internet.

237 Bark With Bite

Catuaba is a small tree found in northern Brazil that locals turn to for a bit of herbal help when they're lacking the energy for a satisfying sex life. The active ingredient, catuabine, is extracted by brewing pieces of the bark into a tonic tea that revitalizes the nervous system and increases sex drive.

250 Lotions And Potions

There's an awful lot of coffee in Brazil—and there's a good deal of guarana, too, which shares many of the stimulating characteristics of coffee. The berries of the guarana yield guaranine, a substance that puts a caffeine-like buzz into your personal relationships. As well as being taken in pill or powder form, guarana is found in many soft drinks, chocolate bars, and chewing gum.

The Apple Of His Eye
The guarana plant gets its name from the Guarani tribe of northern Brazil, who revere the magically restorative property of the berries. One Guarani myth tells the story of the "Divine Child," who was killed by a snake and whose eyes became the seeds from which the plant originally grew.

239 *Puts Hair On Your Chest*

Known locally as "potency wood," the roots and bark
of the muira puama tree are something of a cure-all
to the Amazonian Indians. Infusions are made to
treat indigestion, rheumatism, and even
baldness, but most of all to ensure that
male organs rise to the occasion.
European herbalists also
prescribe tinctures from the tree
in cases of drooping desire, and research is
being done by pharmaceutical companies
into its supposed aphrodisiac power.

Herbalists in the Far East have been using *Tribulus terrestris*, also known as "puncture vine," for centuries. It increases levels of testosterone in the body, giving a real boost to the male sex drive and improving the sperm count, too. Users claim that it works harder and gives a longer-lasting and more intense effect than other aphrodisiac herbs.

Sexual Athletics

In the mid 1990s, Olympic competitors from Bulgaria were being more than usually successful, yet were not failing drug tests. They attributed their exceptional performance to Tribulus, extracted from *Tribulus terrestris*, and word soon got around that it worked for domestic athletics, too.

241 Twice as Nice

The shrub *Piper methysticum*—aka kava, or sometimes "kava kava"—is found growing on may of the islands in the western Pacific. Extracts from the plant form an integral part of religious and cultural rituals throughout the region, as kava induces a state of relaxed euphoria and heightens concentration and stamina—and it has the same effect on the sexual organs.

Chew it Over

Pacific tradition suggests that the kava paste is more erotically effective when produced by virgin girls chewing the root fiber, rather than by grinding it and infusing in water. They may have a point—human saliva does affect the plant's chemical make-up.

Enterprising herbalists in southern Africa have developed an explosive blend of notoriously aphrodisiac ingredients which they call vuka vuka, but is becoming known worldwide as African Viagra. The recipe is, of course, a closely guarded secret, but it is said to contain twenty-one different lust-provoking herbs, including damiana, ginkgo biloba, guarana, horny goatweed, ginseng, maca, muira puama, *Tribulus terrestris*, and yohimbe. That should be enough to raise interest in even the most reluctant members of mankind.

243 Taking Root

Ginseng has been used in Chinese and Ayurvedic
medicine for thousands of years, either in the
form of an infusion or by chewing the raw roots.
Either way—or even in pill or capsule form—it has
proved to be a stimulant to the blood and nervous
system, giving a kick start to the libido. The most
highly prized is Korean or red ginseng, although
Meskawaki Amerindians have also found the North
American variety of the plant effective, especially
when mixed with rattlesnake meat.

Legend has it that the mandrake root, which resembles a little man, screams when it is pulled out of the ground—and that's not the least of its magical powers. It's known in Hebrew as the "love plant," and references to its potency as an aphrodisiac and fertility drug can be found in the Old Testament. As a result, members of the Greek Orthodox church are forbidden to touch the stuff, because "it will lead them into promiscuous ways."

It's Witchcraft

This most potent of aphrodisiac ingredients was used in the preparation of medieval love potions. A root that resembled either a phallus or a woman's body was prized above any other..

245 Clove is a Many-splendored Thing

Cloves are used as both a culinary (*see page 111*) and medicinal spice to perk up the libido, and clove oil is a useful antiseptic and painkiller, often recommended as a salve for toothache. Its mildly anesthetic property has also come in handy as an application for lovers who tend to arrive at their destination ahead of schedule.

Varieties of the passiflora plant, or passion flower, are native to both North and South America, where the leaves and roots are made into potions with antidepressant and analgesic properties. The Indians who first used these brews noticed they also had a rewarding side effect: the passion flower did indeed inflame the passions, and helped men to rise to the occasion, too.

Gay Pride

The Japanese have a slightly different take on the passiflora, which they call the "clock-faced flower." It is not considered an aphrodisiac in Japan, but has recently been adopted as a symbol by the gay community. Perhaps they've discovered its provocative power.

Fit For A Queen

Not a herb, but used in some so-called herbal remedies, royal jelly is said to be health giving and nutritious, especially to the sex hormones. It is produced by bees to feed to their young, and all but one of the hive will be weaned off it before they are fully grown. This chosen one is fed exclusively on royal jelly, which enables her alone to reach sexual maturity, and become the queen who will produce the next generation.

Ambergris is another animal excretion occasionally found in herbal preparations. It's produced in the intestines of sperm whales, probably as a response to irritation caused by the indigestible parts of squids they've eaten, and is found floating in the sea where they have vomited it out. Despite its unpleasant origins, it is said to have aphrodisiac properties; it is probably more palatable applied externally than swallowed.

Use The Gray Matter

Given its provenance and unappealing appearance—it comes in gray lumps—it's surprising that ambergris is so sought after. It is used as a fixative in the manufacture of fine perfumes, and is believed to stimulate the skin into producing attractive pheromones *(see page 330)*.

249 Gotu It!

The fast-growing and vigorous herb *Centella asiatica* is one of many that Chinese herbalists advocate for maintaining youthfulness and prolonging life. Known in Asia as gotu kola or pegaga, it is also believed to maintain a youthful libido and prolong the conjugal pleasures, too.

Another rejuvenating herb is fo-ti—sometimes called fo-ti-teng and ho shou wu—which we know as Chinese knotweed, or more properly *Polygonum multiflorum*. Whatever you call it, Chinese herbalists claim it can more than double life expectancy and restore fertility and sexual desire.

Prime-Time Tale

According to Chinese legend, an old man, well past his sexual prime, was lost in the mountains with nothing to eat but the herb fo-ti. When he eventually got home, his impotence was cured—in fact, his appetite was insatiable and he fathered several children, one of whom lived to be 160.

251   *Gypsy Love*

A philter made from the herb *Veronica officinalis*, or "heath speedwell," is traditionally used as a love potion in Eastern Europe, where some say coyly that it provokes "romantic thoughts." Others are more down to earth about it, and have named the plant gypsyweed, associating it with the stereotypical promiscuity and sultry sensuousness of the Romany people.

Tongkat ali, or *Eurycoma longifolia Jack*, is beginning to catch on in the West, but in Malaysia they've known about its propensity to perk up libidos for ages. Both men and women have found it enhances sexual experiences, and a study at the University of Science, Malaysia, has confirmed its effectiveness, in laboratory animals at least.

It Works Both Ways

Tongkat ali has found its way into the sports field. Athletes and bodybuilders heard rumors of the herb's ability to increase sexual stamina, and found that this was down to testosterone-promoting chemicals in the plant. It is now available as a sort of herbal sports drug.

253 What Is This Thing Called, Love?

Ayurvedic herbal medicine recommends *Mucuna pruriens* for the treatment of several conditions, and the high level of natural levodopa (*see page 291*) accounts for its inclusion as an aphrodisiac. It is also acclaimed as a sexy stamina builder that builds up testosterone levels, often under alternative names such as velvet bean, sea bean, cowitch, yerepe, kapikachu, or atmagupta.

Maca was discovered by the Incas, and the secret of its aphrodisiac potency has been passed down to modern Peruvians. The root is prepared in many different ways, either served as a vegetable, roasted—when it is known as matia—or made into a porridge with milk, or ground into a flour for bread. There is also a beer, chicha de maca, made from fermented maca root.

Winning Ways

Inca warriors used to take maca to give them strength in battle, but the herb was eventually banned by their leaders—not because it didn't work, but because the uncontrollable urges it provoked drove the men to raping the defenseless women of conquered tribes.

255 *Eyes Wide Shut*

Although deadly nightshade is a more appropriate name for this highly poisonous plant, belladonna, meaning beautiful woman, attests to its erotic uses. Extracts used as eyedrops dilate the pupils, as does sexual arousal, making women in particular look more attractive. When applied to the genitals it has a similarly dilating and anesthetic effect, intensifying and prolonging erotic experiences.

Henbane has been an ingredient in magical aphrodisiac brews since the ancient Greeks, and was even found in German beer until it was banned in 1516. It induces hot flushes, increased heart rate, and dilated pupils—just like sex—but the downside is that it's horribly poisonous. That's how it got the name henbane: hens love what it does for them, then they die.

Fly By Nights

The notion of witches riding brooms has some foundation in fact—according to some sources, at least. It was believed in the Middle Ages that witches pleasured themselves with the aid of a mixture of henbane, belladonna, and mandrake on the end of a broomstick.

257 As Easy As ABC

Since they were discovered in the early twentieth century, vitamins have been advocated as the answer to just about every health problem. To some extent that's true, as we need all of them to function properly, but some are especially useful for maintaining a healthy love life. Vitamin A is essential to cell reproduction and development, B1 to circulation and metabolism, C to fertility and stamina, D to hormone and blood-cell production, and E as an antioxidant.

People looking for an aphrodisiac supplement have latched on to vitamin E in particular, and it has become known as the sex vitamin. It seems to have been singled out because it plays an important part in oxygenation of the blood, which rushes to the genitals when you're aroused.

Are You On The Pill?

Although vitamins play a vital role in a healthy sex life—and an extra dose of some could actually improve performance between the sheets—a well-balanced diet and healthy lifestyle should provide all the vitamins you need. Vitamin supplements may give things a boost.

259 Heavy Metal

Oysters are possibly the best-known aphrodisiac food, but what is it that got them this reputation? The answer is probably zinc, which is used by the body for, among other things, producing testosterone. Zinc deficiency often leads to a low sex drive and lack of energy, so taking a zinc supplement may put the zip back when you unzip for action.

Calcium is another important mineral in our diets, essential for formation of healthy bones, and it's that association with hardness that first got people interested in it for improving their sexual standing. But it does play a part in sexual health generally, and is claimed by many to pump up the libido, too.

Elementary, My Dear

Other trace elements that have been found helpful to lovers include phosphorus—although deficiency is rare, and too much damages the kidneys—magnesium for energy and the muscles, and boron, which encourages production of hormones, including estrogen and testosterone.

Sex, Drugs, And Rock'n'Roll

Although frowned upon by most societies, and illegal in many countries, recreational drugs have been used throughout history to enhance erotic experiences: as well as their mood-altering and mind-expanding properties, many also give a sexual buzz. Cannabis, for example, has been used in India as an aid to tantric sex for thousands of years.

Cannabis—aka marijuana, pot, dope, blow, grass, hash, and many other names—is probably the recreational drug most widely used to improve sexual performance. It has the same inhibition-busting and relaxing properties as alcohol, but users claim it has the edge on the booze when it comes to heightening sensations.

The Gravity Of Law

For as long as man—and woman—has been seeking out aphrodisiacs, he's been discovering ways of getting high. Many herbs used to enhance sexual performance also have a narcotic or hallucinogenic effects, and most are legal, while many narcotics enhance sexual performance—yet are illegal!

Raving Mad

Although it has been around since the early part of the twentieth century, MDMA use really began to take off in the 1980s, as an essential part of the rave culture. Originally taken for its energizing effect and the way it can distort perceptions of time, it was also found to alter the way serotonin in the brain controls mood and sexual activity. Users often became more tactile and amorous, hence the drug's nicknames ecstasy (or E) and love beans.

4-Bromo-2,5-dimethoxyphenethylamine is the chemical name for 2C-B, a really potent drug related to MDMA. In small doses it works much the same as ecstasy—but anything over about 15 milligrams (0.0005 ounces) and it induces psychedelic hallucinations that could very well disrupt rather than intensify any lustful activities.

Sounds Like Fun

Mood-altering drugs have an odd side effect on some people. They can induce synesthesia—which means, for example, music is heard as colors, or physical sensations perceived as sounds or visions. This may enhance lovemaking—or the user may not know whether he's coming or yodelling.

Not To Be Sniffed At

Glamorized by its many celebrity users, cocaine is extracted from the South American coca plant, and made into a powder which is usually snorted into the nose—often through a rolled high-denomination banknote. This frequently causes spontaneous sexual arousal, helpfully combined with a boost to energy and stamina levels.

Hitting The Spot

Because coke temporarily numbs mucous membranes before making its way into the bloodstream, some users found that applying it to their genitals rather than the nose made lovemaking a longer-lasting and more intense affair.

Speed—to give it its street name—pretty well sums up the effects of amphetamine: a rush of energy and alertness that can last for hours, and increased blood pressure, temperature, and pulse rate. It's been a favorite amongst heavy rock bands since the 60s, inspiring several songs that confirm its sex-and-drugs-and-rock'n'roll status—such as Canned Heat's *Amphetamine Annie*, with its ironic chorus of "Speed kills."

267 *Going Down On You*

Horses for courses, I guess, but tranquilizers and barbiturates don't suit everyone—although some users claim they promote languorous lovemaking. They're depressants designed to reduce anxiety and tension, and were thought to be pretty hip in the beatnik era, but perhaps the cats back then had, like, more sexual hang-ups.

A favorite for thousands of years, the extracts of the Oriental opium poppy induce feelings of euphoria and contentment, and all pain and discomfort just melts away. In this dreamlike state, almost everything is a pleasurable experience, and erotic feelings are said to be intensified—but users are often so self-absorbed that they miss out on those particular joys.

A Smack In The Kisser

Opium derivatives, heroin and morphine, go by numerous different names (from horse through junk to smack), but are equally addictive and could end up replacing rather than enhancing sex.

The Acid Test

Endorsed by a whole generation during the 1960s, LSD—lysergic acid diethylamide, or acid—was the key to the ultimate psychedelic experience. Changing the way the senses perceive just about everything, an acid trip is a mood-altering, mind-bending adventure that could add a new dimension to making love. However, LSD is also notorious for bad trips, so this is one mind-bending adventure you should consider giving a miss.

Who Wants A Toad's Tool?

Several fungi contain powerful hallucinogens, either psilocybin or ibotenic acid. These substances distort perceptions in much the same way as LSD, but almost invariably induce a euphoria. Users of these "magic" mushrooms also claim to enjoy things more intensely, including sex.

Works Like A Dream

The British writer Aldous Huxley described his experiences of mescaline in the books *The Doors of Perception* and—more tellingly—*Heaven and Hell*; Derived from the peyote cactus, mescaline is reputed to give the user mystical hallucinogenic visions. Like other psychedelic substances it can make a mundane love life a dream, or transform it into a nightmare.

271 Party Poppers

The group of stimulants that includes amyl nitrite, butyl nitrite, and isobutyl nitrite are known colloquially as poppers. They come as a liquid, in bottles or small glass phials, which evaporates at room temperature. Inhaling the fumes gives an instant and alarming rush of energy, accompanied by sudden loss of inhibitions and sexual arousal. Alas, this can only be a quick fix though, as the effects last a matter of minutes.

As well as it's use in Tantric rituals, the ancient Indian tradition of Ayurvedic medicine prescribes cannabis as an aphrodisiac. It comes in many forms, the best known of which is *bhang*, a sweet drink made from cannabis leaves and flowers, milk, sugar, cardamom and other spices, which is reputed to increase libido, promote healthy erections, and aid lubrication—in short, cure all sexual ills.

Bedded Bliss

Traditions of cannabis-based aphrodisiacs exist in many cultures. Brides in nineteenth-century Serbia were served *nasha* on their wedding night— a less-than-exotic mixture of cannabis and lamb's fat.

Just What The Doctor Ordered

Conventional medicine and pharmaceutical companies tend to be a bit sniffy about the claims made for traditional and illicit aphrodisiacs, but they're just as keen to find really effective remedies for disappointed patients. The scientific approach has had some success, too, especially with drugs such as Viagra, whose results seem to stand up to scrutiny.

Once upon a time, in a country far away—China actually—there was a goatherd who noticed his flock were more than usually horny after they had eaten a weed growing in his fields. He decided to try the horny goat weed for himself—it worked, and the rest is history. We know it today by the name Epimedium.

The Old Ones Are The Best

Scientific tests showed that horny goat weed actually does make you horny, so pharmacists gave it a fancy Latin name, and suddenly we've got a new wonder drug on our hands.

Snow White And Happy, Doc

The jury's still out on this one—at least as far as the U.S. Food and Drug Administration is concerned—but medics are getting excited about the use of Bremelanotide, formerly known as PT-141, to increase sexual arousal in both men and women. It was discovered by chance during research into a drug to help people tan without the dangers of ultraviolet light. As a tanning aid it was a failure, but none of the subjects of the test cared, as their libidos were racing.

One drug that's been a prominent success is sildenafil citrate, better known as Viagra, now available on prescription and, less officially, from suppliers all over the world. It's reckoned to be successful for around 70 percent of men with problems of rigidity, but sorry, there's nothing similar yet for the ladies—although they say a hard man is good to find.

Hard-hearted Treatment

Viagra was found by accident. Pharmaceutical companies working on treatments for angina noticed sildenafil citrate had a beneficial effect on the male patients, and not where they had expected. Plan B was immediately adopted, and professional reputations were secured.

277 It's In The Blood

The dilation of the sex organs depends on adequate blood flow, which is, in turn, affected by nitric oxide (NO) in the body—with me so far?—and arginine, a naturally occurring amino acid, controls our production of NO. So, it follows that a supplement of arginine will help stimulate and maintain sexual arousal and increase sensitivity. It's that simple.

Hydraulic Rams

It depends what you're expecting from medications to improve sexual function, but some express disappointment when they find they're capable, but still not enthusiastic. As one clinical psychologist put it, most of these drugs are "about the hydraulics of sexual performance, not the desire."

Now, where arginine gets the physical side of things sorted, another amino acid, levodopa—or simply l-dopa—works on the psychological side. It promotes production of a chemical called dopamine, which affects the way the brain controls our moods, movement, and sexual behavior. L-dopa can help boost sex drive and desire, which in turn speeds up arousal, and increases the frequency and intensity of orgasm.

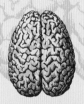

Come On Wake Up

A report in the *Canadian Journal
of Psychiatry* tells the story of the
discovery of the climactic effects of the
drug Anafranil: some patients reacted
to the drug with uncontrollable yawning,
followed by spontaneous orgasm;
in fact, even deliberate yawning
would bring them to a climax.
Boredom can be fun.

Come-pulsive
Unfortunately, Anafranil doesn't work for everybody—in fact, it's a fairly
uncommon side effect of the drug, which is used to treat depression and
obsessive-compulsive disorder. But if you're one of the lucky ones you'll
find the orgasms coming thick and fast.

Actually, a number of antidepressant drugs are claimed to have aphrodisiac effects on some users. Imipramine, for example, has recently been in some demand on the strength of rumors that it will work wonders on the libido. It's not yet clear whether there's any truth in this, or whether just pulling out of depression reawakens an interest in sex.

Come Off It

One of the more unfortunate side effects of heroin and cocaine abuse is a loss of libido. The drugs bromocriptine and naloxone were developed to help wean users off their addictions, and in the process no doubt helped to restore their interest in sex. This got them something of a reputation as aphrodisiacs, but they're really only useful for those trying to kick a habit.

A couple of treatments used for Parkinson's disease—pergolide and amantadine—are also arousing some interest in sex-therapy circles. They don't actually have any effect on the libido, but have apparently proved useful in cases of anorgasmia, the inability to reach a sexual climax.

Bringing It Off

Research into the function of the neurotransmitter serotonin showed that it has a negative effect on sex drive. Subsequent tests using P-Chlorophenylalanine to block the serotonin in rats had a positive result: the males displayed an increase in sexual activity—but only among themselves.

Is That Really Necessary?

Another substance being researched as a medical cure for our sexual failings is dehydroepiandrosterone (DHEA). Put simply, it's the stuff our bodies use to produce hormones such as testosterone and estrogen. It's produced from cholesterol by the adrenal glands, sex organs, and other cells—and you thought that stuff was bad for you! Without it, no sex hormones and no sex. OK?

Upjohn's Caverject—the unlikely name given to a form of prostaglandin E1—holds the honor of being the first prescription drug for the treatment of male impotence. It came into use in 1995, and was originally injected into the penis, but a microsuppository version, designed to be inserted into the urethra, appeared the following year.

A Seminal Matter

Despite the name, prostaglandin is not secreted by the prostate gland, as was thought when it was first discovered in seminal fluid in the 1930s. In fact, it comes—quite literally—from the seminal vesicles. So now you know.

Heady Hormones

Oxytocin is a hormone released into the body during orgasm in both sexes, but is also produced during childbirth and breastfeeding—so it probably has more to do with sexuality in women than men. It is thought to have an effect on the psychological as well as physical aspects of mating in general, and could play an important role in sexual desire.

Counterintuitively, the group of drugs known as alpha blockers, which are used for lowering blood pressure in cases of hypertension, have been shown to promote the flow of blood when injected into the penis, and they stimulate firm and long-lasting erections. Makes you wonder who found out, and what he was doing ...

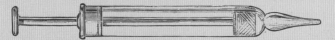

The Proof Of The Put-in

A dramatic demonstration of the potency of alpha blockers injected into the penis was given at a meeting of the American Urological Association in 1983. A certain Dr. Brindley, having self-administered the treatment prior to his lecture, dropped his pants to show his audience the successful result.

It'll Make A Man Of You

Although testosterone is normally associated with all things macho, and adult men produce about twenty times as much of this anabolic steroid as adult women, it's important to health, and in particular to sexual health, in both sexes. Among other things, it drives libido and physical energy, so a dose could improve a flagging sex drive.

Quite a Build-up

Anabolic steroids, both natural and synthetic, help the body to build muscles and increase strength and stamina, so it's not surprising that some athletes like them. But use, or abuse, of these so-called sports drugs is not confined to track and field—sexual performance is enhanced by them, too.

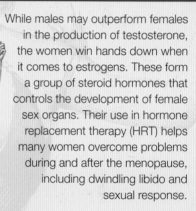

While males may outperform females in the production of testosterone, the women win hands down when it comes to estrogens. These form a group of steroid hormones that controls the development of female sex organs. Their use in hormone replacement therapy (HRT) helps many women overcome problems during and after the menopause, including dwindling libido and sexual response.

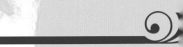

289 Mind Over Matter

The role of sexual psychology is often overlooked in the search for ways to improve our love lives, but it's just as important as the mechanics of lovemaking. Aphrodisiacs that simply stimulate the physical organs aren't going to do much good on their own if the desire isn't there, and counseling or therapy could be the answer in some cases.

Don't Be A Freud

It all goes back to Sigmund Freud, really. His theories that sex is at the root of, well, just about every problem have influenced us for nearly a century. Your lack of libido, or unsatisfactory performance in bed, goes back to childhood repression, he stated, and only psychotherapy can put it right.

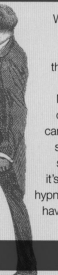

When psychotherapy was in its infancy, hypnosis was widely used to get patients to reveal their unconscious thoughts and sometimes to implant ideas. Nowadays, some practitioners claim that hypnotic suggestion can help psychosexual problems such as lack of libido and even some cases of impotence, but it's probably a myth that you can hypnotize someone into letting you have your wicked way with them.

When all else has failed—pills, potions, injections, and psychiatry—medicine has looked toward engineering for solutions: for stiff problems, try tough answers. The first attempts to find a surgical remedy for lack of rigidity were pioneered in the 1940s, and involved the transplanting of cartilage splints from other parts of the body. The techniques were refined over the next decade or so, and acrylic implants were introduced in the 1950s.

Now abandoned, one "cure" for erectile dysfunction, also touted as a penis enlarger, involved the use of a vacuum pump. The device created a vacuum around the penis, sucking blood into it and creating an erection that could be maintained by a tourniquet to stop the blood rushing back out again.

Quantity, Not Quality

Size is not important we're told, but judging by the number of remedies for penis enlargement on the Internet, people don't believe that. Most of them are rubbish, of course, but there are some surgical techniques for underdeveloped or reluctant organs that can help in extreme cases.

The Perfumed Garden

A more direct route to a man's—or a woman's—heart might be through the nose. There's evidence that scents work more effectively than edible aphrodisiacs. Some aromas invoke memories; others stir up a sense of anticipation, stimulating sexual arousal. Whether you choose massage lotions, aromatherapy oils, room-fragrancers, or incense burners, scents are very personal, so prepare to experiment.

Deerly Beloved

True musk comes only from a gland in the male musk deer, but other animals, as well as some plants, produce a similar substance containing the essential ingredient, muscone. The musk deer secretes this stuff to send out an olfactory message that he's in charge, and the strong-smelling scent derived from it is thought to act like a pheromone (*see pages 330–31*) in humans, too.

Roses are inextricably linked with love and romance, and are a perennial favorite on Valentine's Day. Their scent warms the hearts of the women, rather than stirring up lust, but apparently works the other way around on the guys: rose oils and perfumes are believed to mimic female hormones, making the girls gooey but the boys boisterous, so present your boyfriend with a rose bouquet.

He Rose To The Occasion

Roses have been a sign of true love as far back as classical times, when they were considered the sacred flower of Aphrodite. Confirmation of their use to seduce comes from Cleopatra, who had her room strewn knee-deep in rose petals and invited Mark Antony back to her place—evidently it did the trick.

295 *It Goes On And On*

You either love it or hate it, but patchouli is one of the strongest and longest-lasting of all perfumes. The scent is unmistakable, and its lingering quality is symbolic of stamina—when it works it is said to be one of the most potent perfume arousers. So good, in fact, that it's used as an ingredient to give body and staying power to a lot of fine perfumes for both men and women.

Summer Of Love

In the West patchouli had its heyday in the 1960s when no self-respecting hippy would be without it. The whole love-and-peace thing caught on to its aphrodisiac powers, probably through growing interest in Indian culture and religion—the god Krishna is thought to manifest himself in patchouli.

Aromatherapists believe that sandalwood oil has a soothing, calming effect and strengthens the yang energy (masculine, active) to enhance enjoyment of physical pleasures. For perfume makers, sandalwood provides a good base for their products. But all you need to know is that it stimulates the libido—sandalwood incense in the bedroom creates a really amorous atmosphere.

The Hills Are Alive

The delightful scent of lavender is almost overpowering in the hills of southern France, where it is grown commercially, so it might be the place for a restorative holiday if your love life's on the wane. Lavender's strong, heady smell has been found by Chicago's Smell & Taste Treatment and Research Foundation to provoke greater sexual arousal than almost any other scent—the winner, oddly, was pumpkin pie. Freud would have a field day.

A Good Rubdown

298

Although its aroma is quite subtle, the shrub myrtle is deceptively potent. Its essential oils provoke positive reactions in both sexes, and when mixed in olive oil make a balm or massage oil that is far from calming—especially when rubbed on by your partner.

Myrtle Is Fertile

We're back to the Doctrine of Similars *(see Introduction)* with myrtle, as it first got noticed by the ancient Greeks when they realized the fruit resembled a clitoris. Because the fruits and oils lived up to expectations, it was declared sacred to Aphrodite and brides often wore crowns of myrtle branches.

The Perfumed Garden 313 ♥

299 *Love In A Cold Climate*

Ylang-ylang grows in the islands of the Pacific Ocean, and oils derived from it are used by the locals to calm anxiety, lower inhibitions, and generally put them in the mood for love. It has only fairly recently been discovered in the West, where perfumiers and aromatherapists are finding the sweet, exotic scent brings on tropical torridness in more temperate climates, too.

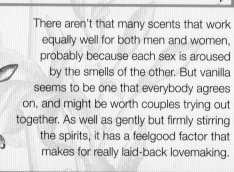

There aren't that many scents that work equally well for both men and women, probably because each sex is aroused by the smells of the other. But vanilla seems to be one that everybody agrees on, and might be worth couples trying out together. As well as gently but firmly stirring the spirits, it has a feelgood factor that makes for really laid-back lovemaking.

Good Enough To Eat

Vanilla is well known as an aphrodisiac food, too (*see page 120*), and it is possibly its associations with comfort foods such as ice cream and desserts that give the scent its warm glow. Use it as a perfume, though, especially as an all-over body spray, and you'll stimulate a different kind of appetite.

A Good Lei

The flowers you usually see in those Hawaiian necklaces, called leis, or behind the ears and in the hair of other Pacific islanders, are hibiscus blooms. They're not only gorgeously bright and blowsy, but also have a sweet and heady scent. Locals say that coffee made from the seeds pumps up the passions, but just a whiff of exotic hibiscus is often enough for most people.

The intense and exciting bouquet of jasmine is used in many perfumes and sometimes to give an extra dimension to the aroma of some foods and liqueurs. In aromatherapy it is said to induce confidence and optimism as well as lust, so it could work well for men who need a little encouragement in coming forward.

Sex Symbols

Across Asia and the Pacific, hibiscus and jasmine have symbolic significance. They are the national flowers of many countries in the region, and play an important part in many of the cultural and religious ceremonies, especially weddings and fertility rites.

303

Sheikh, Rattle, And Roll

The dried resin of the *Commiphora myrrha* tree, found in East Africa and southern Arabia, is used in perfumes and incense. Myrrh, as we know it, is notoriously expensive, but its rich aroma more than compensates for the cost. Traditionally used in the Middle East in an anointing oil, it was thought to be the height of sophisticated sexiness—and it might evoke some of the atmosphere of the harem for you.

Another resinous perfume from the Middle East is frankincense, which, as its name suggests, is burned as incense. The oil, however, is also used in aromatherapy and perfumery and has a reputation for stimulating and rejuvenating when and where it's needed most.

Fit For A King

You might be wondering why it was that the Three Wise Men brought frankincense and myrrh as well as gold at Christ's nativity. Well, it's probably because they were expensive gifts, and considered fit for a king.

305 Fruitful Fragrance

Not that many people have even heard of bergamot—and those that have usually only know it as the stuff that gives Earl Grey tea its distinctive bouquet, but it's also used in eau-de-Cologne for its refreshing and invigorating zest. Derived from the peel of fruit from the tree *Citrus bergamia*, the essential oil perks up the sex drive and has all the sweet, orangey scent you need to get you feeling fruity.

The essential oil of clary sage—*Salvia sclarea*—is highly recommended by aromatherapists for women suffering the effects of PMT or the menopause, as they believe it works to balance out the female hormones. Even if you're not having any of those troubles, it's still pretty useful, as its estrogen-like qualities are also said increase sexual appetite and stamina.

No Laughing Matter

There's a bonus with clary sage oil. In addition to giving the sex drive a nudge, it has a slightly narcotic property, too, inducing a feeling of relaxed euphoria and heightened sensitivity. Put some of this into an incense burner, and suddenly everything's a pleasure, even to the point of hilarity.

Keep Off The Grass

Several fragrant grasses yield essential oils that are much used in perfumery as the base of many scents. Some of these, lemon grasses such as citronella grass and palmarosa, for example, have been thought of as having aphrodisiac qualities, but it is the closely related vetiver that leads the field in that respect, producing woody, masculine scents with a touch of lemon that women find particularly arousing. An added bonus is that its earthy character means men can wear it with confidence.

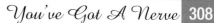

Cedarwood oil is one of the oldest of the essential oils, and was used by the ancient Egyptians both medicinally and cosmetically to arouse and attract their lovers. In aromatherapy it is considered revitalizing and confidence building, and helps encourage interpersonal interrelation—which, I suppose, is a roundabout way of saying that it gets you horny, and it gives you the nerve and energy to do something about it.

Love You To Death

The ancient Egyptians noticed another side to cedarwood. The timber itself is quite impervious to rot, so made good coffins, and the oil extracted from it has preservative properties—useful for embalming mummies. Hence it came to be associated with death as well as sex. Don't let that put you off.

Libido Lifter

Almonds have been linked with love and fertility in many cultures, and both the *Kama Sutra* and *The Perfumed Garden* mention them as a passion-provoking food (*see page 70*). Oil extracted from the almond tree has a very distinctive, nutty scent that has the same effect on female libidos as the nuts themselves, and in Ayurvedic medicine it is considered more stimulating to women than nibbling the nuts.

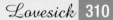

The heady perfume of narcissus flowers can be pretty overpowering, and it will drive you crazy—either with lust or, I'm afraid, nausea. People react really violently to the scent one way or the other, so it pays to do a bit of preliminary investigation before trying it out. The one to look out for is known in perfumery as jonquil, made with the essential oil of the Narcissus jonquilla.

Self Love
Pliny explains the derivation of the name Narcissus as coming from the Greek narkao, "to make numb," from the heavy aroma of the flower. He was probably wrong, however, it is more likely named after the mythical Greek youth Narcissus who fell in love with his own reflection.

311 Happy Together

Sometimes referred to as the flower of collective happiness, the mimosa is the source of a rich and floral scent that is reputed to promote psychic dreams. If that's true, you'll know that you're in for a good time when you use some to get the evening going your way—mimosa perfumes are also sensual and arousing.

Sense And Sensitivity

An interesting attribute of many plants of the mimosa family is their sensitivity to touch and heat, earning them the nickname "sensitive plant." Run your finger over the leaves, and they fold up as if they've been tickled—which is perhaps a sign of what it can do for your love life, too.

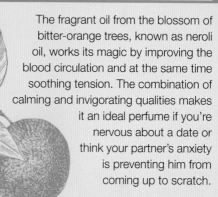

The fragrant oil from the blossom of bitter-orange trees, known as neroli oil, works its magic by improving the blood circulation and at the same time soothing tension. The combination of calming and invigorating qualities makes it an ideal perfume if you're nervous about a date or think your partner's anxiety is preventing him from coming up to scratch.

313 Light The Touch Paper

So sensitizing is the oil of the lemon verbena herb that the International Fragrance Research Association recommends not including it in perfumes to be used on the skin. However, it's fine to use it in an aroma lamp, which can fill a room with its uplifting citrus scent, encouraging you and your lover to explore a truly tactile experience.

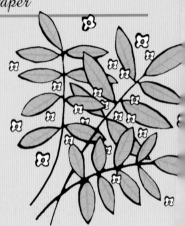

Another of those smells you either love or hate, the scent of violets is either an instant turn-on or a short cut to a lonely night. The essential oil is extracted from the leaves of the plant, as the scent of the flowers has a peculiar quality: after the initial rush of fragrance, it desensitizes nasal receptors, temporarily disabling the sense of smell.

Advice From The Shrink

The phrase "shrinking violet" to describe a shy person comes from the plant's habit of protecting itself from harsh sunlight by growing toward the shade. If you subscribe to the theory of treating like with like, violet-leaf oil might be the answer for those who lack the confidence to make the moves.

315 *Love Is In The Air*

Now, these are the things that really hustle up the hormones—pheromones. While other scents might mimic their effect, these odorless chemicals are the real thing. Women produce pheromones called copulins that can cause a surge of sexual response in men who get a whiff of them, and the androsterone produced by men has the same impact on women.

The chemical compounds that make up human pheromones have been isolated and even synthetically produced, so perfume makers are enthusiastic—as are their customers—about the potential. There are already dozens of perfumes on the market using both natural and manmade pheromones, with startling claims for their effectiveness—but don't get too excited about getting them excited: it's still pretty much in the experimental stage.

Not Everybody's Got What It Takes

If you're hoping that pheromones will make you irresistible to the object of your interest, unfortunately there is a slight drawback ... Both copulin and androsterone are detected by a special receptor in the nose, the vomeronasal organ, but it appears that not everyone is blessed with this handy detector.

It's been said that men sweat, women perspire, and ladies glow. Whatever you call it, to a lot of people sweat is sexy. After all, getting hot and wet is what sex is all about, and the most erotic images are often of bodies glistening with perspiration. It's not only a symptom of arousal, however, it can be its cause, as sweat actually contains a good helping of pheromones.

Identity Theft

The gladiators of ancient Rome were the beefcakes of the age, bringing on hot flushes in the females in the amphitheater. Less macho men, in the hope that some of these obvious attractions would rub off on them, would go backstage to buy some of the gladiators' sweat to use as a body lotion.

"Home in three days. Don't bathe," was the gist of Napoleon's letter from the battlefield to his beloved Josephine. Apparently, he found her natural odors more stimulating than the smell of soap—and maybe he had a point. If you want your pheromones to get things going for you, it makes sense not to wash them all away—unless, of course, you're a pig farmer or sewage worker.

319 Good Clean Fun

A good way of preparing yourself for a hot date—unless you're meeting Napoleon *(see previous page)*—is a soak in the tub, and it's also an opportunity to slap on some smellies. Choose soaps and bath oils with sexy scents—it'll put you in the right frame of mind, arouse your lover's interest, and maybe you'll come out of the evening smelling of roses.

Not everybody is turned on by natural body smells, and let's face it, some people are really not nice to know when the heat is on. Using a deodorant is more than just a cover-up measure and can really freshen up your partner's interest, too. An appropriately aphrodisiac fragrance will make you nicer to know when the heat is on and could even enhance the effect of any pheromones you're producing.

How Do You Like It?

Without wishing to go into too much personal detail, there are a number of areas of the body that can benefit from deodorant application. Where? Well, there's the joke about the drugstore assistant selling deodorant to a foreign customer: "Aerosol or ball?" he asked, and got the reply, "No, underarm."

321   *Don't Breathe A Word*

Don't overlook the small details when you're preparing to get up close and personal. You might think you've got it all covered by spraying on the stimulating scents and burning incense for incentive, but it'll all fall apart if you've got breath like a dog. Minty mouthwash is a bit clinical, so look out for old-fashioned floral sweets or lip-gloss with fruity flavors to make your mouth more inviting.

The ancient Greek physician Galen had some strange ideas, including the notion that erections were a result of bodily gas—which might have influenced his thinking on what constituted aphrodisiac food. If you follow his advice about beans and cauliflower, for instance, then get hold of some flatulence-reducing remedy, too, or all your perfumed preparation will have been in vain.

The Top And Bottom Of The Problem

A fair number of aphrodisiac foods give rise to unwanted consequences, so plan your menu to avoid obvious gas producers. And, although it's probably OK if you're both eating something that lingers on the breath, think twice about a cheesy, garlicky, or fishy snack before meeting your date.

Gentle

Encouragement

Whether you're trying to entice a new love or to rekindle the fire of an existing one, relying on aphrodisiacs alone will not guarantee success. The art of seduction takes skill, and certain techniques need to be learned and practiced. This final section contains morsels of miscellaneous advice on ways to bring your lover to his or her knees, from playful persuasion to frolicsome foreplay.

323 *Whatever Are You Suggesting?*

Don't overlook the power of suggestion when you're making your play. In medicine its known as the "placebo effect"— essentially, if the patient believes something will work, then it will. If you can subtly imply that what you're giving your lover will have the desired effect, you'll more than likely achieve the desired result. It helps if you have faith in it as well, of course.

Nothing Does It Better
"The sole love potion I ever used was kissing and embracing, by which alone I made men rave like beasts and compelled them to worship me like an idol." ANONYMOUS SIXTH-CENTURY ROMAN COURTESAN

If you believe in that sort of thing, you could get a bit of help from the supernatural. We're not just talking voodoo dolls and mystical incantations here, or even love potions and philters. What about astrology, for instance? Consult your horoscope—and your lover's—to see if it's a good time to take the plunge.

Spell It Out

To ensure your date reaches a satisfying conclusion, carve your and your lover's names into a candle with a pin, rub rose oil into the names, and light, all the while concentrating on how you'd like things to turn out.

325   *The Feeling's Mutual*

If you're anticipating a night of passion, the last thing you want is a headache—especially if it's your lover who's got it. Make sure that it doesn't happen by suggesting a massage to soothe away the tension. It's a wonderfully sensuous way to relax, and the tactile activity will almost inevitably continue beyond the merely therapeutic.

A session in the gym will get you fighting fit for any bedroom athletics. Not only that, it'll get you in the mood too: working out, jogging, and all forms of exercise release feelgood chemicals called endorphins into the brain, improve circulation to every part of the body, and increase levels of testosterone. And regular exercise will give you the stamina to go on and on and on ...

The Games People Play

It's even better if you can work out with your lover before you make out. Noncompetitive activities you can do together—such as swimming, horse-riding, or cycling—will get you both hot and work up your appetites, but it's probably best to avoid competitive games, especially boxing.

Choosing what to wear for a date can make all the difference, giving you more confidence but also signaling seductive intentions. For women, low-cut, backless, strapless dresses and high heels all arouse interest, while men do well in something close-fitting. Clothes that reveal just enough of your charms will invite curiosity and encourage exploration—and remember, what goes on may come off, so sexy underwear may be the clincher.

Make Up Your Mind

It's a matter of taste, of course, but looking your best usually involves a bit of aid from cosmetics. Heavy mascara and eye liner will help achieve that come-hither look, and lipgloss hints at the labially luscious delights on offer, but it's up to you how far you go, especially on a first date. And for the guys? At the very least a shave, and maybe a haircut, unless you're sure she goes for the Cro-Magnon type.

The Best Is Yet To Come

It's not just what you put on, but what you take off—and how. Show your hand (or anything else) too soon, and you lose the effect. Take a tip from the professionals when it comes to stripping for action: a little at a time is more tantalizing, and the anticipation can be almost unbearably arousing.

Gentle Encouragement

There are whole books devoted to explaining the language of flowers, but the message comes over loud and clear if you take some along for your date. It's a traditional token of love, and these days even men appreciate the gift of a bouquet. Roses are an obvious choice, but other flowers have seriously seductive scents, too. Go easy if you use them as table decorations, though, or you'll spend the entire meal craning your necks to see each other.

The other, rather corny lover's gift is a box of chocolates, but even their infamous power of arousal could be bettered. Jewelry might melt hearts, but it's tricky to get right—too expensive and it looks like bribery. It's the thought that counts, so your gift should reflect what you're actually thinking: sexy clothes, for instance, which you can offer to help put on—and take off.

A Girl's Best Friend
"I have always felt a gift diamond shines so much better than one you buy for yourself."
MAE WEST, ACTRESS

Pure Romance or Porn?

The sexes are, generally speaking, divided on ways to woo: women are moved by the romantic, men turned on by the pornographic. If you can find the middle way, then you're on to a winner—when the opportunity arises, some mildly erotic literature or images, such as the *Kama Sutra*, may have you both up for the same thing.

Eye Of The Beholder
"The difference between pornography and erotica is lighting."
GLORIA LEONARD, EROTIC ACTRESS AND MAGAZINE PUBLISHER

Toying With Your Affections

A whole range of inventive products is available under the headings marital aids or sex toys at certain specialist stores. There's something for everybody, whether they tickle, vibrate, wobble, or clench, and they add an extra dimension to your love life or get it going when all else fails. It's beyond the scope of this little book to go into too much detail, but suffice to say they'll have you in fits of either ecstasy or laughter, and there's no doubt they'll break the ice.

333 *Hideous Kinky*

We're getting into deep water here, but you might find that your lover— or maybe even you—needs an extra little something to get things going. With some people it's shoes, or uniforms, or an unusual location, with others it's an element of humiliation or domination, but whatever it is, don't worry, fetishes are not uncommon. Just remember the anonymous adage: "Erotic is when you use a feather. Kinky is when you use the whole chicken."

It's difficult to be yourself when you're nervous about the way the evening's going. One way around this is to indulge in a bit of role play with your partner. Try playing prostitute and client, gigolo and client, master and slave-girl, or whatever fantasy takes your fancy.

Strike A Pose

"I've tried several varieties of sex. The conventional position makes me claustrophobic and the others give me a stiff neck or lockjaw."

TALLULAH BANKHEAD, FILM ACTRESS.

335 If You've Got It, Flaunt It

When it comes to attracting the opposite sex, fame and fortune work better than almost anything else—just ask any celebrity or millionaire. But where does that leave us lesser mortals? Well, it may sound corny, but being generous and proud of what you have got goes a long way—and you won't get pestered by gold-diggers.

All You Need Is ...
"Power is the ultimate aphrodisiac."
HENRY KISSINGER—but he doesn't make it clear whether it turns him on or other people

However you plan to persuade, tempt, or allure someone—and whatever wiles you use to arouse them—it's going to entail some verbal as well as physical communication. Between the initial chat-up line and the final invitation, if you can keep the conversation flowing you're more likely to get the juices flowing, too. A sense of humor helps, as does being a good listener, in making a smooth transition from social to sexual intercourse.

Risk is a turn-on for many people, and the higher the stakes the more they like it. Some get their kicks from gambling, so a day at the races or a night at the casino could be a prelude to a dead cert. But why not combine the pleasures—for the risk-takers the mere suggestion of an illicit affair or sex in a public place is enough to drive them wild.

Get It Out In The Open

"I don't mind where people make love, so long as they don't do it in the street and frighten the horses."
MRS. PATRICK CAMPBELL, BRITISH STAGE ACTRESS

Actually, there's almost nothing that doesn't arouse somebody, somewhere, sometime. There are a few things that still take us by surprise, though, especially in well-established relationships when we might think the spark has gone for good. And if arousal catches you unawares, so much the better—have you noticed, for instance, how making up after a serious row often ends up with the best sex in ages?

339 Before The Foreplay

If you're serious about seduction, a bit of forward planning won't go amiss. Simply downing a few oysters or spraying on the pheromones won't get you anywhere on their own. Whether it's a night on the town or a cozy evening in, give yourself plenty of opportunity to ply your date with suitably sexy food and drink, and a chance to check they're having an effect. You're hoping to build up to the big climax, remember, and a series of little nudges in the right direction are going to work better than a big shove.

That all-important first date can be a nerve-racking experience, but the pressure's off a bit if you go to a show. Cinema, theater, and concerts are all good ways of enjoying something together, and the seating encourages intimacy. And even if the show's awful, it'll give you a starting point for conversation.

Too Much Information

Check the program carefully before getting tickets to a show. A friend of a friend took his date to see a movie called *Public Enemy Number One*. It turned out to be a documentary on sexually transmitted diseases.

Feeling Good

The food, drink, and romantic atmosphere all play their part in getting your partner in the mood for some erotic action, but there's no substitute for physical contact. Just brushing past when serving the dishes, or touching hands across the table will do for starters, followed by playing footsy— surreptitiously touching feet and legs can lead to all kinds of under-the-table activity.

Gentle Encouragement

The turning point in most dates is when it comes to the first kiss. Shifting gear from a chaste peck through the lingering embrace, to a full-on French kiss can move your lover's thoughts from saying goodnight to having a good night. Kissing is the foreplay to the foreplay, and your lips and tongue can be very persuasive.

More To Come

"Now a soft kiss—Aye, by that kiss, I vow an endless bliss."
JOHN KEATS

343 *Making A Meal Of It*

A time-honored way to treat your date is to meet up for a meal. Taking someone out to dinner signals your intentions to some extent, and offers an opportunity to try out the effectiveness of some of the aphrodisiac foods, too. A classic table for two in a candle-lit restaurant is a safe choice for seduction, but you could be more adventurous and opt for a sexy sushi bar.

Cocktail Clincher 344

Show over? Dinner finished? The night's still young, and you're not yet ready for bed, so it's time to check out a bar or club somewhere. This could be the clincher if you handle it right, and a couple of drinks will help things along. There's nowhere else to go from here, so it's make or break time, and the adrenaline levels are often high enough to kick the passions into play.

345 *Are You Sitting Comfortably?*

Sooner or later you're going to want to invite your lover to your place, and you'll need to create the right atmosphere if you're hoping for more than just a cozy meal. You also need to think about where you're going to entertain—facing one another at the table, but near enough to touch if the occasion arises, and somewhere comfortable to relax after the meal, with no choice but to sit close together.

There's a subtle difference between romantic and gloomy lighting, and you want to be able to see each other and what you're eating. Candles are always a winning detail, and cast everybody in a more flattering light. Pools of light also draw the two of you in, like moths to a flame, and encourage an atmosphere of intimacy.

Blind Date

"Many a man has fallen in love with a girl in a light so dim he would not have chosen a suit by it." MAURICE CHEVALIER

Background music can set the mood for the meal, so choose carefully—music works on the emotions more than the brain, and often has emotional associations. Couples usually have a song that they consider their "tune," bringing back some fond memories, but if you're doing this for the first time it's best to pick something slow and schmaltzy, at least to start off with. Save the heavy stuff for when things are getting livelier.

Food Of Love

If music be the food of love, play on;
Give me excess of it, that, surfeiting,
The appetite may sicken, and so die.
WILLIAM SHAKESPEARE, "TWELFTH NIGHT"

It Takes Two To Tango

George Bernard Shaw once said that dancing is the vertical expression of a horizontal desire. It's a sort of mating ritual for most of us, and an invitation to the dance floor could give you the break you're after. Even the most energetic disco moves get the blood pumping and lower the inhibitions, but it's the body contact of the slow numbers that starts the smooching.

Your mind might be on which seductive meal you're going to serve when you invite someone over for dinner, but try to think foreplay here. Play it cool: pour a couple of aperitifs and settle down with some aphrodisiac hors d'oeuvres to tantalize the tastebuds and stimulate the appetite.

Bon Apetit
"L'appétit vient en mangeant."
(The appetite grows by eating.)
François Rabelais, "Gargantua"

Presentation is everything when you're cooking something up to impress. Arranging the table with care is important, and may be something you can share with your guest, but ultimately it's the food that counts. It's in the nature of many aphrodisiac dishes, such as asparagus and oysters, to look the part and invite eating with the fingers, and serving some of these suggestively shaped foods clearly should get your message across.

Of course, it may be you who's been invited for the meal, and you are, in effect, playing an away game. The rules are similar, but the tactics are slightly different. To ensure you don't have to find a ride home, don't forget to take a gift and compliment everything that's put in front of you. Flattery never fails—nor does offering to do the dishes, or suggesting it can wait until morning.

It isn't easy encouraging the hots when you're not calling the shots. If your host is the one who's a bit backward in coming forward, you have to show more than just your appreciation to get them off the starting blocks. Working on the principle that nothing succeeds like success, nothing arouses like arousal: let them know that their efforts have had the desired effect in affecting your desires.

Web Designs

"Will you walk into my parlor?" said a spider to a fly:
" 'Tis the prettiest little parlor that ever you did spy."
MARY HOWITT, "THE SPIDER AND THE FLY"

353 *Lip Smacking*

When planning a meal or choosing from a menu, go for at least one thing that's either dripping with butter or oil or so full of juice that you'll need a napkin. Foods like that can't be eaten demurely, and the sight of moist lips and even a little dribble down the chin will probably get your partner salivating, too.

... it's the way that you eat it. A dinner date is a good opportunity to share food with your lover, and spoon-feeding each other with a luscious dessert or, even better, popping fruit into one another's mouths with your fingers, with your eyes closed to heighten the tactile and taste sensations, should bring the meal to a climax.

Good Taste

"Many so-called aphrodisiac recipes are basically wholesome ingredients prepared in a tasty way. The receptivity to romance probably comes from the general sense of relaxation and well-being good food induces."

HARRY E. WEDECK, LINGUIST, CLASSICS SCHOLAR, AND AUTHOR

Nothing beats getting away from it all for stepping up the pace of a new relationship or revitalizing an older one, and taking off for a weekend together is almost always a recipe for increasing the excitement. You've got a couple of days to get to know each other better, the chance of at least one seductive dinner, and a night or two to put it all into practice.

From the moment you check in—especially if you sign the book as Mr. and Mrs. Smith—hotels start to work their magic and create a honeymoon atmosphere, or perhaps a second bite at the cherry. After all, what they provide is food, drink, and bedrooms—all surefire aphrodisiacs. There's only one thing that could let you down: twin beds.

Do Not Disturb

So you've checked in, got to the room, and unpacked. It would be a shame to miss an opportunity to start the ball rolling, so ring room service and get a bottle of bubbly and some tantalizing snacks sent up, and you won't have to leave the room until breakfast.

357 A Vacation Romance

Now, if a weekend away gets your lover in a lather, just think what a week or two could do. Freed from the ties of work and schedules, you can devote yourselves to pleasure, and take your time over it, too. Different vacations suit different people, but whether it's a stay in a luxury hotel, touring, cruising, or even camping, the fun won't stop at the end of the day.

Taking a longer break means you can broaden your horizons and choose from all sorts of exotic and erotic locations—and maybe revisit some old haunts that have kindled your passions before. It could be that cabin in the mountains with the prospect of some après ski, exploring a romantic city, or just basking in the sun with a drink by the pool—just take your lover to places that they want to go to.

Love In A Hot Climate
"What men call gallantry, and gods adultery,
Is much more common where the climate's sultry."
LORD BYRON

359 Rub A Dub

It's always good to relax in the tub or take a refreshing shower, but twice as nice if you've got company. If you can entice your partner into the bathroom to share the experience, working up a lather together is bound to lead to a more invigorating scrub.

Even if your tempting tactics have done their work, and you've managed to pep up the passions enough to move the action from the dining-room to the bedroom, it's no time to turn off the heat. To keep your lover simmering, your boudoir should have more of the honeymoon suite about it than the bachelor pad, from lighting to linen.

First, Make Your Bed

Whatever you're thinking of doing in the bedroom, it's been done before. In London in the seventeenth century, an inventor called John Graham set about making a bed that would "arouse all who rest thereupon," and came up with one that had lights, music, and incense to set the mood.

361 *How Was It For You?*

Mission accomplished, and hopefully a satisfactory result for all concerned, but why let it end there? You could well wake up with an appetite for a second helping, but not without a willing partner. Now's the time for a restorative breakfast of fruit juice, eggs, toast, and coffee to wake up the libido again—and, of course, it's best served in bed.

The Morning After
"The thing women like best in bed is breakfast."
ROBIN WILLIAMS

It's been assumed that you're aiming for a night of ecstasy, but we shouldn't take that for granted. Daytime lovemaking is fun, too, outdoors if the weather's good. To fuel the fires and set the scene for some alfresco antics, take a trip to a secluded spot and treat your lover to a lunchtime picnic. The afternoon should look after itself.

363 | *Where Do You Want It?*

Postprandial passion needn't mean a move to the bedroom—there are plenty of other places you can get it on. Suggest doing it right there in the sitting-room, or even the kitchen, and the urgency of your passion could work wonders. In fact, sex somewhere out of the ordinary might be the key to turning your lover on.

Gentle Encouragement

Some lovers love to play, and the whole business of seduction is the game they enjoy most. For others, games are part of the serious business of seduction. A bit of healthy competition and an element of gambling add spice to the libido. Strip poker (or even checkers or chess) should liven up the evening, or if you prefer something a bit more physical, Twister™—or make up your own variations of children's games such as blind man's bluff.

Mind Games
"Games lubricate the body and the mind."
BENJAMIN FRANKLIN

365 Playing Hard To Get

Don't give up hope if you seem to be getting nowhere; it may be that you still haven't found the right buttons to press. For some, particularly men, the pleasure's in the chase, and the ultimate turn-on is tantalizing temptation. So, coming on strong is going to be counterproductive with guys like that, and the less interest you show, the better it gets for them.

Makes The Heart Grow Fonder

"Absence diminishes commonplace passions and increases great ones, as the wind extinguishes candles and kindles fire."

FRANÇOIS, DUC DE LA ROCHEFOUCAULD

And last but not least, if you want to know for certain what will make your lover weak at the knees, try asking outright what it is that really turns him or her on. As well as getting a few useful pointers for future reference, the question could spark off a conversation that gets both of you going!

Acknowledgments

The publishers would like to thank the following
for permission to reproduce their images:
Corbis: DK Limited/Corbis page 98; TopFoto: page 267;
Getty Images: Walter Simbal/StockFood Creative page 26